*A candid view of life as a female trucker
on the highways of Great Britain.*

PROLOGUE.

So, what's it like being you?

Unsurprisingly, this is the question I am most often asked when a new acquaintance learns of the nature of my occupation. Mostly, my reply would be short and dismissive, something along the lines of "Oh, it's just a job like any other" and to an extent that would be true. There are good days and bad, moments when you are blessedly free to enjoy a great song on the radio, or a good audio book accentuated by the beautiful backdrop of our ever-changing countryside. There are other days when a four-hour wait at a depot with few comforts or facilities yawns like a great chasm ahead of you, particularly when it is 1 am, you have no internet signal, and that four-hour wait is followed by a three-hour drive back to your depot and another one-hour drive in your car to get home.

I began my driving career at the tender age of twenty-one following an eventful year as a dark-room technician for a local regional newspaper during which time I made several lifelong friends among the photographic fraternity and several short term enemies within senior management, something that appears to be a running theme throughout my life.

Finding myself made rather acrimoniously and unceremoniously unemployed and accepting a job as a van driver for an engineering firm in Bristol, I relocated away from my hometown with the intention of searching for work more closely aligned with my goals.

Those particular goals remain to this day, rather tragically unrealised.

Instead, I discovered the joy of the open road and the freedom of a working life not constrained within four dull walls capped off by a hanging ceiling full of harsh fluorescent lights all flickering in time to the rhythm of my soul being slowly strangled.

Since those long distant days, I have worked for more than ten agencies, been contracted to more companies than I can actually recall, and undertaken work as mundane as delivering food and as unconventional as delivering fire engines. Over a decade ago, I worked for two years as a trade-plater, a unique occupation and something of a dark art in which hitch-hiking around the country was considered to be part of the job. I have hauled for most major and some minor supermarkets, many of the most well-known retailers, and several builders merchants amongst others.

It should also be noted here though that I am something of an accidental trucker. As a child, I

wanted to work with animals and become a veter-
inarian. Several failed CSE's later, which included
a grade four in arithmetic, that's *arithmetic* mind
you, mathematics was completely beyond me, I
came to understand that this particular ambi-
tion was probably not within my grasp. After a
brief foray into painting and decorating and another into photography, as previously mentioned,
my newly acquired vocation as a professional
driver saw the tools of my trade slowly ascend-
ing from small vans into larger vans, small trucks
into larger trucks until finally culminating in
eight tonnes of Volvo FH followed closely behind
by eighteen intimidating tonnes of double-deck
trailer with a maximum overall weight of forty-
four tonnes, including the load.

Occasionally, boredom or frustration with
my reluctantly chosen career has diverted me
onto other paths and into other countries but for
never longer than two years at a time before I have
dragged my sorry arse back into the world of un-
social hours, late nights, early starts and an ever
diminishing social life.

I have observed with delight as trucks have
evolved from the dirty, noisy, spine-jarring wrecks
of the late nineties into the clean, smooth tech-
nologically advanced behemoths of the present
day. From eighteen manual gears in a crash gearbox (upon which I have played many an unhappy
tune) to four simple buttons on the dashboard
(drive, neutral, reverse, and a manual override).

From broken tape cassette players to Bluetooth accessed music and voice-activated dialling. From blind-spots you can lose a small crowd in, to mirrorless vehicles (the mirrors being replaced by rotating cameras which feed four internal screens) and all-round motion sensors.

No doubt autonomously driven trucks will be the next great advance in the field of transport and logistics, eliminating the need for a qualified and experienced driver at the helm and along with that need will vanish a wealth of knowledge and a rich history of a life less ordinary. There are those amongst my peers who learned the trade on their father's knee and who mourn the loss of the manual gearbox and the advent of the mobile phone when drivers assisted other drivers and each man, and they were mostly men, knew how to rope and sheet or change a wheel and could think of themselves as more than 'steering wheel attendants'.

I came to truck driving at the age of 28 in the late 1990s and do not miss those times one little bit. I am reassured by the knowledge that my depot is open around the clock and that help is never more than a phone call away. I do not miss driving filthy trucks, full of rubbish and stinking of cigarette smoke and the previous drivers' late-night curry. I have no hankering for manual gearboxes and ludicrously stiff clutch pedals that cause one's left leg to ache for days after making deliveries in London during rush hour. I anticipate, with great relish, the day that I am handed the keys to my first fully electric articulated vehicle. I am also sadly aware that I am in the minority. The average age of a truck driver in this country currently stands at forty-eight. That is the *average* age, meaning of course that many are far older. The oldest I have heard of recently celebrated his eightieth birthday.

Ours is a dying trade and advances in technology will probably be the final nail in the coffin of every lorry driver still working today so if you have purchased this book with thoughts of beginning a career as a truck driver it would be wise to remember that it may not be for ever or for everyone. That said, it has served me well thus far and I continue to prefer it over almost any other form of vocation, so with this book, I hope to inform the uninitiated, amuse the enlightened and empower those who wish to walk in the steel toe-capped footsteps of the British trucker.

So sit back, enjoy the journey and if you are still smiling when you get to the end, it may be time to dust off that CV, dig out your licence, and Google for a local instructor. I promise you won't regret it!

IN DEMAND

Currently, the UK is experiencing a 75,000 driver shortage. [Please note - since the conception of this book, which took only nine months to write, this number is now estimated to have increased. For more information, see epilogue]. This is evident in the number of hours each driver has to work in order to cover demand. Drivers' regulations are exceptionally complex, whole tomes are written on the subject but the long and short of it is that in the space of a seven day period you can drive for six days, nine hours each day, increasing to ten hours on two of those days making a maximum total of 56 driving hours in a week. Over the course of two weeks, you cannot drive for more than 90 hours and you must take a 45-minute break after 4 hours 30 minutes of driving or a 30-minute break after 6 hours of working (whichever comes first).

So, let's put this into perspective. A truck is limited to a maximum of 56mph in the UK. Were it possible to drive 837 miles from Land's End to John O' Groats entirely at this speed without stopping (which it is not, so don't try it) then a truck driver could make the equivalent of this journey almost four times in a six-day week. Think of the furthest car journey you have ever undertaken and how you felt once you had arrived at your destination. No doubt you were exhausted, stiff, bored, and glad to be out of your car where you could stand up, stretch or perhaps then settle into a comfortable sofa or a warm bed with a hot meal inside you. No such luxuries in store for the truck driver. A hot meal maybe but the only bed on offer may well be the bunk in their truck and the location nothing more inviting than a noisy layby. All this can be followed up by a paltry nine hours of daily rest on three nights a week. On the remaining nights of that week, the driver can enjoy a comparatively lavish eleven hours of rest each night, followed by an alternating cycle of one or two days of weekend rest.

To many, this regimen would appear extreme and truth be told, many drivers would not be expected to work to their maximum permitted hours, day in, day out, every working week. However, a fifteen-hour day, ten hours of which could be spent behind the wheel traveling up and down the motorways of Great Britain would leave anyone exhausted. Add to this the arduousness of nighttime driving during which the white lines on the road can quite literally hypnotise you into a stupor and the fact that a moment's lapse in concentration can at best find you riding the rumble strip bordering the hard shoulder and at worst

dear old 'mother nature' in the form of mud and dust.

Several years ago, I used to daily perform a trailer swap at a depot in Nottingham. This involved taking an unloaded double-deck trailer (a very tall trailer with two floors inside it) to the site, uncoupling it from the tractor unit, leaving that trailer in its parking space, and coupling up to a loaded trailer before returning to my own depot in Bristol. This particular depot in Nottingham had two trailer parks. One was beautifully tarmacked with well-spaced and well-marked parking bays and the other was, well, little better than a swamp in winter and a dustbowl to rival the Sahara desert in summer.

Frequently I would be asked to use this dreaded place, usually following a morning during which I had paid particular attention to the cleanliness of my cab. Once I had left that site with my return trailer heading for Bristol, you could be fooled into believing I had not cleaned the truck for weeks. If we had experienced a long period of hot, dry weather, the dashboard would be coated in a fine, gritty dust which found its way into every crease and crevice of the trim. Conversely, if the weather had been wet and cold for some considerable time, the floor of the cab, the door panelling, the steering column, and the front of the driver's seat would be covered in a viscose layer of mud that had adhered itself to my trouser legs and been tracked into the cab on the soles of my boots in impossibly thick and sticky clumps.

On more than one occasion the hazardous nature of that mud had seen me slip-sliding in comedic fashion around my vehicle whilst performing my walk-around-checks. I'm glad to report that it never quite got the better of me, though I heard that other drivers working that site had not always been so fortunate.

It takes most new drivers less than a year to develop a sense of 'resigned stoicism' towards the total disregard with which our needs are catered for when it comes to assisting us to operate effectively in our work and to live as dignified human beings (as would be considered the right of any other member of the human race). These needs include, though are not limited to:

Adequate numbers of clean toilet and shower facilities which are accessible 24/7.

Adequate parking for trucks at a reasonable cost (£30 per night is not reasonable)!

Lorry parks and haulage yards which are not dangerous, muddy, flooded, unlit, or poorly marked.

Delivery points which are readily accessible and unobstructed by skips, pallets, and parked cars.

Waiting times to load or unload which do not stretch into half a day.

Access to nourishment not limited to a vending machine full of crisps and chocolate.

Simply addressing these salient points nationally, persistently, and uniformly would make a huge difference to the everyday life of the truck driver and perhaps even work effectively in attracting much-needed 'new blood' to the game.

THE LAND OF NOD

According to recent statistics, it is thought that driver fatigue accounts for up to 25% of fatal or serious accidents per year with 40% of this figure involving commercial vehicles.

What is more surprising and shocking, however, is that most drivers, upon hearing those statistics would probably remark "Is that all"?

It is a damning commentary upon this industry that four out of every ten fatigue related incidents on our roads involve a commercial vehicle.

Most drivers, myself included, have experienced both insomnia whilst trying to sleep and extreme tiredness whilst driving a truck, resulting in some fairly unorthodox techniques for remaining alert (drinking ten cups of coffee in a single night, opening truck windows in sub-zero temperatures, singing to extremely loud music and literally slapping oneself in the face) coupled with some truly bizarre techniques for ensuring restful sleep. These can include but are not limited to: The use of eye masks and earplugs, vigorously exercising directly before retiring to bed, herbal sleeping draughts, hot baths, and open windows even in the dead of winter to increase the flow of oxygen in the bedroom. Personally, I find the use of Valerian along with Vitamin B complex and calcium and magnesium most beneficial but everyone is different.

Sedatives, illegal substances, and alcohol have also been used by some, as goes without saying though (and I cannot state strongly enough here) this is most definitely ill-advised if one wishes to retain ones' licence, liberty, and life.

Exhaustion is the greatest battle fought by any truck driver. Deadlines? Pah! Traffic? No problem? Adverse weather? A breeze! Resisting the overwhelming desire to sleep whilst driving a truck at 2 am along a quiet motorway? Now that's a challenge!

How many of you reading this book have settled down into a comfortable easy chair of an evening, in a warm, dark room and drifted off to sleep in front of the TV? Well, driving a warm, comfortable truck at night along endlessly straight roads has much the same effect. Daylight is easier, it's more natural for the human body to be alert during the day but at night that same body wishes to betray you. It doesn't matter how much sleep you have had during your rest period, when the sky darkens, we are all inexorably drawn towards our beds!

Some drivers do manage to adjust and nighttime work becomes easier for them, but many do not, and their rest periods become peppered with bouts of insomnia and other sleep disorders. We are after all, not machines and it would be wise for the haulage industry to remember that.

For those of us who return to our depot every night, there is then the commute home. There have been many occasions when I have actually been unable to remember much of my journey between leaving the depot and arriving at my front door. There have been many more near-accidents on my commute home than I would care to admit to and moments when I have drifted onto the hard shoulder or veered off towards the shrubbery only to jolt myself awake at the last possible second. What is most alarming is that I am not alone in this.

It is not for no reason that truck drivers pay a very high premium for car insurance, on average around 30% more, and though there are companies who specialise in insuring the private vehicles of truck drivers they are few and far between.

For those of us who spend the week in our vehicles, only returning home at the weekend, there are other issues. The greatest challenge being, finding somewhere to park for the night. Drive around the lorry park of any motorway service area of an evening between Monday and Thursday and you will find it usually find it full to the gunwales with sleeping truckers. Occasionally our vehicles will be overflowing into the coach park, car park, and onto the approach of the slip road. To say that this country is deficient in parking spaces for trucks would be understating the facts. On any night, more than 18,000 trucks will be parked up but with only 15,000 spaces nationwide, where do the remaining 3,000 go? Drive past any layby on a trunk route or take a late-night excursion to an industrial estate and you will find your answer.

Do these drivers receive adequate rest? Of course not! Could you sleep with other vehicles thundering past your bedroom, mere feet from your head at night causing your bed to rock in the backdraft? I think, you have your answer.

Obviously, overnighting in lay-bys and industrial estates is far from desirable. Without any toilet or washing facilities or access to refreshments of any kind, the life of a trucker can often be somewhat undignified.

Some companies do provide showers for visiting drivers but these are disappointingly rare. Even motorway service stations usually provide no more than one or two showers to be shared by every driver in their lorry park. If the lorry park is particularly large, this can be well over 50 drivers, all wanting access to the same space at approximately the same time, leading to filthy facilities and queues out the door.

This is where the female trucker can fare a little better with cleaner, less frequented facilities though I have more than once visited a motorway service area which did not provide any showering facilities for women whatsoever and with most motorway service areas charging more than £30 per night just to park, you would imagine they could at least provide clean showers in sufficient quantity. To add insult to injury, the lorry park is often situated as far away from these facilities as it is possible to get, making any late-night visit to the little boy's (or little girl's) room, something of a midnight excursion. For most men, the rear wheels of their truck become a makeshift urinal, for girls, the option is a bucket in the cab or the ground beneath their trailer. This is why lorry parks smell so badly in the summer. That is the smell of enlarged prostates and quiet desperation.

Truck-stops are of course are always going to be the best option but these are harder to find and becoming fewer in number with every passing year. They usually provide an abundance of clean and well-maintained facilities, they often charge less for the privilege and the food served is of better quality and more affordable. The only issue is that all truck drivers know this and as a consequence, they are the first parking places to be filled of an evening. Arrive late to any truck stop on a week day and the chances are that you will be turned away at the gate.

There is of course the issue of safety when it comes to finding a place to park for the night. Theft from trucks in lay-bys is not an unusual occurrence as it would be hard to distinguish the movement of the load from the backdraft of passing vehicles rocking your cab.

A former colleague of mine actually had his entire fuel tank unbolted and removed one night when he parked in a layby. Fuel theft is common, the curtains on curtain-sided trailers are routinely slashed so that the potential thief can view the contents, and hundreds of trucks are hijacked in any given year for their loads (which can be worth in excess of £1,000,000 per fully loaded articulated vehicle). The hijacking itself is often done at knife point.

But not all overnighting experiences are alarming for truckers. Some are amusing, confusing, or just plain odd. One particular night spent in a motorway service area springs to mind. It was around 9 pm when I received a knock on my cab door. I drew back my curtain and opened the window to a young woman who was dressed for more clement weather than a British winter would provide. Her purpose was clear and I was not of the gender she was expecting. To this day, I am still unsure as to which one of us was most surprised to see the other.

I am also reminded of the predicament once faced by a former colleague of mine in the 1980's. To spare his blushes here, let's simply call him Frank. He had arrived late to a truck-stop in an area he was unfamiliar with and had just managed to grab the last available parking space. He struck up an idle conversation with the driver in the truck to the left of him and discovered that he knew the area well. The driver then asked Frank if he would like to accompany him to the local pub for a hearty meal and half a beer. Frank enthusiastically agreed and they developed quite an amiable friendship during the course of the evening.

During their time in the pub, the wind had picked up significantly, so fearing rain, upon their return, they hurriedly parted company and climbed into their respective vehicles. Frank was aware that his driver's door had a sticky catch and would occasionally lock itself unexpectedly. To remedy this situation, he usually left his passenger door unlocked so that should this happen, he would be able to get back in. However, on this night he locked both doors because he was leaving the vehicle unattended and after returning to the vehicle, neglected to unlock it again.

Once he was inside, undressed, and with that half-pint of beer finally making its winding way towards his bladder, he realised that he needed to make a trip to the little boys' room. Remembering that the facilities were at the far end of the lorry park and noticing how his cab was swaying in time to the howling gale, he decided to water his rear wheels rather than run across the lorry park to the toilets. This would not have been an ill-advised decision had he decided to put some clothes on. So, in his birthday suit, he exited from his vehicle and walked along the length of his trailer towards the rear of the truck. He was just finishing off his business when he looked up in time to see a particularly vicious gust of wind blow the driver's door closed.

Remembering he had locked the passenger door earlier in the evening and with a sinking feeling in the pit of his stomach, he raced back to the cab and tried the door. Predictably, it was locked.

The result of that predicament saw him politely knocking of the window of the truck next door in the hope that his new acquaintance would have something with which he could break the quarter light window so that he could get back in (this was in the day when trucks actually had quarter light windows). Heaven knows what his new 'pub buddy' thought as he stared down at a man he barely knew, standing naked at the door of his truck wearing nothing but a pair of rigger boots and a hopeful smile on his face.

A THIEF IN
THE NIGHT.

As previously mentioned, theft is a serious problem for haulage companies, their clients, and the drivers responsible for delivering the goods safely.

Road freight crime costs the UK economy in the region of £250,000,000 per year.

The nature of this crime mostly involves theft, which in itself, can take several forms, the most disturbing of which involves the hijacking of the vehicle. This usually entails the driver being held at knife-point or gun-point and being forced to either hand over the keys to his vehicle so that it can be driven away, or being made to stand by whilst a criminal gang opens the trailer doors and unloads the goods from the vehicle then and there. Occasionally, the driver may have his vehicle boarded and be forced to drive it, along with its cargo to an unspecified location whereupon the theft will take place.

If the driver is fortunate, he may be left restrained but otherwise unharmed, however, incidents resulting in aggravated assault or even death of the driver are not unheard of.

For anyone who works in the retail sector, the months approaching Christmas are the busiest time of the year. Drivers are flat out during these times, desperately trying to keep up with demand as the general public hits the stores and their credit cards with wild abandon. From September to December, the number of trucks on UK roads hits its peak and all available overnight parking bays in truck-stops and motorway service areas quickly fill. Anyone late to the party will often have to settle for a lay-by or a lonely industrial estate and these are where many incidents of theft and hijacking occur.

Motorway service areas too are sometimes targeted and even truck-stops are not immune. Those without floodlights, security barriers, secure fencing, and state-of-the-art CCTV may be targeted.

However, the most common type of cargo crime (over 60 percent of theft in a typical year) involves the 'slash and grab' approach. This is where the curtains of the curtain-sided trailer are slashed open with a sharp implement and the goods are stolen straight off the deck. Quite often the driver knows nothing about what is happening to his vehicle and continues sleeping, oblivious to the destruction. The truth only becomes apparent when he exits his cab in the morning to find his curtains in tatters and his trailer empty. The value and 'portability' of the load is also a deciding factor. An articulated vehicle full of sheet steel is obviously far less likely to be targeted than a cargo of laptops. A prime example of this is evident in the recent hijacking of an articulated vehicle full of Apple computers with an estimated value of over £5,000,000 an incident during which both the driver and the security guard on site were forcibly restrained but otherwise unharmed.

LGV drivers are not the only targets of this type of crime. Those who deliver high-value goods to domestic homes can also be targeted. In my early years as a driver, before I acquired my LGV licence, I remember listening in to a conversation on a handheld short wave radio between one of my fellow couriers and an office-based member of staff. The conversation went something like this:

Dave: "Dave to base one, come in base one".

Base one: "Go ahead, Dave".

Dave: "Got a bit of situation here base one. I can't get back into the van."

Base one: (Chuckling) "Why's that Dave, you locked yourself out"?

Dave: "No mate. As you know, I'm on the Hartcliffe run today and it's a bit of a rough area right"?

Base one: "Yes Dave, we know that, what's the problem"?

Dave: "Well, I don't know if this is normal but

I've just made my delivery and returned to the vehicle to find some angry bloke with a chainsaw cutting a hole in the side of my van".

Base one: (Pause) "Well bloody well stop him"!

Dave: (Very long pause) "Which one of the words 'angry bloke with a chainsaw' did you not understand"?

There are of course other types of LGV vehicle crime. One of these includes the "Flash for cash" scam. This involves flashing the headlights at a truck driver indicating that he should pull out. The truck driver then proceeds to pull out and the individual who 'flashed' them, deliberately drives their car into them. That person then claims on the insurance of the haulage company both for damage to their vehicle and for personal injury. This is similar to the more common 'Crash for cash' scam in which a car driver overtakes an LGV and once in front, hits the brakes hard. Quite often, the driver of the car will have removed the brake light bulbs on his vehicle prior to attempting this type of fraud, resulting in the LGV driver rear-ending the car with potentially catastrophic consequences.

In recent years, many haulage companies have fitted their vehicles with front and rear-facing cameras in the hope of preventing such incidents but they do still occur. There have also been incidents where individuals have fabricated entirely fake damage claims to their vehicles simply by noting down the registration numbers and details of LGV's visiting a certain area and claiming that their vehicle was clipped by the truck as it passed their stationary car.

Any one of these scams can be hard to disprove without camera footage and many companies pay out rather than endure a protracted and expensive court case. This of course raises the insurance premium of the haulier and that additional cost can eventually travel in only one direction. That's right, you guessed it! Straight on to the consumer.

I'm relieved to say that in all my years as a driver, I have only once been the subject of vehicle crime in the form of fuel theft.

As a trade-plater, it was not uncommon for me to have to leave a truck unattended at night since many of the vehicles I moved around the country were municipal vehicles, contained no bunk, and were therefore unsuitable for an overnight stay. In the case of several refuse vehicles I delivered, they were so foul that you were tempted to check yourself for parasites upon disembarking, and consequently, overnighting in the fetid stench that filled the cab would not have been considered by even the most hardcore of trade-platers.

This particular evening I was driving a vehicle from somewhere in Essex to the outskirts of Leicester for delivery the next morning. Since the truck did not have a sleeper cab (a legal requirement for taking ones daily rest inside the truck) I had booked myself into a B&B for the night, conveniently situated within walking distance of the industrial estate where I parked.

Upon returning to the vehicle, I was somewhat alarmed to find that the fuel gauge, which had shown as half full the night before, was now barely reading above the red line. It was my first and only experience of fuel theft and it took a little while for the penny to drop and for me to realise exactly what had occurred.

There was, however, one occasion I can recall when the skills of an experienced thief came to my rescue. I was working for a well-known parcel company and had to make a delivery to a prison in the centre of Bristol. The van I was driving that day was fitted with slam locks upon the rear doors and as I was leaving the prison, one of the guards closed the back doors of my vehicle whilst the keys were still in the ignition and I was standing behind it. After much deliberation, an inmate was employed to break into the van and deliver us both from a very embarrassing situation.

One of the funniest stories ever recalled to me was of an incident regarding a retired gentleman and his much-loved motorhome which was kept on his driveway at night when not in use.

One morning, the day after returning from holiday, he stepped out of his front door and was surprised to find a pile of vomit on his driveway next to a jerry can and a rubber hose extending from one of the outlets of his Motorhome.

His initial confusion with the situation was soon replaced by a dawning realisation which was then supplanted with glee once he understood exactly what had happened.

It appears that an opportunistic criminal had attempted to siphon diesel from the fuel tank of the motorhome by using his mouth to suck the fuel up the hose so that it would then flow freely from the tank and into the receptacle he had brought with him.

Fortunately for the motorhome owner and unfortunately for the budding thief, instead of selecting the inlet for the fuel tank, he had selected the outlet for the chemical toilet which was still full to the brim from the owner's recent trip. I cannot vouch for the validity of this story but it is truly a perfect tale of instant Karma and amused me so greatly that I felt compelled to include it. Sorry!

On a more serious note though, there are many areas of the UK where commercial vehicle crime is an almost daily occurrence. The worst hotspots appear to be centred mainly around Northamptonshire and the West and East midlands. For female truckers, in particular, this could be an area of serious concern and personal safety may be one of many reasons why women are deterred from choosing haulage as a career.

Simple precautions though such as opening your roof hatch at night rather than a window in hot weather, removing all visible items from the dashboard, and ensuring your doors and fuel cap are locked can all help to prevent theft and attack. Women, in particular, should never park alone overnight, should always make themselves known to their fellow truckers and they should certainly never announce their overnight location publicly on social media along with details of the load they are carrying.

Drivers carrying immovable goods (such as sheet steel) should open a trailer door at night to prevent 'slash and grab' incidents and those carrying high-value goods should never park anywhere that is not fully secure. As a female trucker who is no longer required to do a night out, whenever I need to answer a call of nature, I would rather pull into the fueling area of a service station than be forced to tramp across an unlit lorry park at night. Fueling areas are always bristling with CCTV cameras which view the driver and vehicle from almost every angle. As all truckers, sooner or later are forced to conclude, the life and safety of a driver is worth far less to some than the contents of his fuel tank.

SECOND CLASS CITIZENS

As I have previously touched upon, truckers are not treated too well in this country. On the continent attitudes towards drivers are far more favourable. In many European countries, overnight parking is free and readily accessible. Facilities are clean and numerous and the driver is treated with a level of respect which almost borders upon reverence. This cannot be said of the British trucker.

In recent times with the outbreak of Covid-19, truckers have been the grateful recipients of a new and welcomed level of appreciation. As key workers, we are invaluable, keeping the country moving, delivering essential goods in uncertain times.

However, this unexpected outpouring of goodwill is unlikely to last, neither is it likely to change the lot of the average trucker. It may make us feel better about ourselves (everyone loves to be appreciated, right)? But the reality is that to most car drivers, we are often thought of as a menace on the roads or an inconvenience, slowing down the journey of the harried commuter.

When the general public thinks of a trucker, they imagine someone middle-aged, overweight, unwashed, and smelling of cigarettes who cares little for their lorry, their cargo, or the queue of vehicles trailing behind them on a busy A-road in rush hour and whilst there is always some truth clinging stubbornly to that stereotype, many of us bear little resemblance to that cliché.

We are professional men and women, we are not our vehicles or our cargos. We are not the dirt on our boots or the grease on our hands. We are not the rain-drenched roads upon which we travel at night or the dirty showers we are forced to use in the mornings. We are not the filthy toilets or the watery, lukewarm coffee that we paid too much for. We are not the re-heated ready-meal or the late-night phone call to family we have not seen in days. We are not defined by our work any more than anyone else is though because of our work we are often treated as though the job itself is all that we are.

It can be said that some of us are a little rough around the edges but that salty humour often stems from a darker truth and that truth is that our work is hard.

The hours are long and unsociable. We experience little human interaction throughout most of the day. We are often isolated and must rely upon our own initiative to solve problems.

The work can be physically demanding and mentally draining. We get tired, sweaty or cold and often very, very wet and dirty! Far more is expected from a trucker than almost any vocation for which a university degree is not required.

Our responsibilities are terrifying, the demands upon our time and commitment, seemingly boundless and every day we transport all of the cargo that eventually finds its way into every factory, business, and home throughout the land. The value of our vehicles can be compared to the price of a three-bedroomed house, our load can be valued in the millions and yet we continue to carry this burden of responsibility along with additional knowledge, that should the worst happen, we can be killed or suffer life-changing injuries on any given day, simply by doing our jobs.

A recent incident which ran for more than a week over the Christmas and new year period saw thousands of truck drivers stranded along the M20 in Kent whilst thousands more were herded onto a local airfield when a new strain of Covid-19 instigated a UK-France border closure.

Operation stack was created in 1988 but has been most intensively used since 2015. It is implemented whenever the amount of freight using the UK to France channel crossing routes becomes limited due to adverse weather, strikes, or port or tunnel closures. This will see the M20 and other motorways in the surrounding areas closed to all but those using the channel crossings. During these times, these motorway routes, which can hold around 3,000 trucks, become used as lorry parks along with Manston airfield which can hold a further 4,000 vehicles.

Facilities for both of these options are minimal, to say the least. Many drivers reported a lack of available food and water along with no facilities for showering and wholly inadequate facilities for washing and toileting. Some were using the wheels of their vehicle, others were finding relief in the surrounding fields, hedges, and ditches.

Taking the mathematical view of this situation, assuming one person for every vehicle and ignoring the fact that some of these vehicles would be double-manned, that's 7,000 people making at least five toilet stops per day. That's 35,000 'deposits' of human waste per day, 15,000 of which would be deposited along 40.2 miles of road with one toilet every kilometre. That's 70 toilets for 3,000 drivers, each toilet receiving 214 'deposits' per day (that's once every 6.7 minutes in case you are wondering, barely enough time for a satisfactory evacuation in my humble opinion). For the 4,000 drivers at Manston airfield, it was several days into this scenario that a further 70 toilets arrived on site adding to the 80 already there, raising the total to 150 toilets on site to cope with 20,000 'deposits' per day making it 133 'deposits' per toilet, per day. These would all, of course, be temporary toilets of the 'Portaloo' variety.

During a brief Google search, I came across a portable toilet calculator (yes, that is actually a thing) and used it to find out how many toilets should have been provided if Operation Stack was actually a construction site (meaning that the toilets would not have been emptied every day, as was no doubt the case). The recommendations were alarming. One hundred toilets for every one thousand drivers bringing the total to 700. This is what should have been provided. What was actually provided was, at best, a total of around 220 toilets, approximately one-third of what should have been, all this before we even consider the food and drinking water situation.

It is recommended that every individual should consume around 2.5 litres of water per day, for 7,000 drivers that equates to 17,500 litres of water, that's more than one 30,000 litre water bowser every other day for drinking water alone.

As for food, 7,000 drivers would consume 21,000 meals per day, probably more than all the fast-food outlets in the area combined could possibly provide.

In this situation, many members of the local community stepped up to the plate, providing 8,400 meals for stranded truckers, delivering curry and pizza to waiting drivers, in some cases, lowering food bundles on rope from the motorway bridges to hungry men and women below. These wonderful acts of kindness warm my heart greatly though the mathematics alone goes to prove that whilst this supremely generous effort on the part of the general public was no doubt greatly welcomed, it was a drop in the ocean compared to what was required to tackle the vast scale of the problem. A problem which should not have to rely on local good-will for its resolution. This was a local issue which should have been handled on a national scale, though I do not anticipate governmental attitudes towards my fellow truckers changing permanently any time soon.

It isn't just the hearts and minds of the public we need to win over, it is the hearts and minds of those who make the laws and those who grudgingly provide us with the type of filthy, inadequate, and unfit-for-purpose facilities that you wouldn't expect any other kind of self-respecting human being to use. I have been told many horror stories relating to lack of clean or even available facilities. One tale passed on to me was of a fellow driver, so desperate for the toilet whilst delivering to a site close to the water at night, that he sent a 'depth charge' of the brown variety over the edge into the waters of the Manchester Ship Canal.

I was also told of another chap who used to make regularly deliver huge, open-topped bags of building sand to various sites in the UK. He soon discovered that in a desperate situation, he could climb onto the back of his truck and use his cargo like a form of human kitty litter and no one was ever the wiser for it.

Female truckers in particular can find themselves at a great disadvantage when it comes to toilet provision. I would frequently arrive at a delivery point outside of normal working hours to find that the only female toilet available would be locked for the night and therefore all but inaccessible. Consequently, I have frequented more gentlemen's toilets than I would care to admit to, none of them pleasant I hasten to add. It would also be pertinent to mention that drivers of both sexes are regularly refused access to toilet facilities. On what grounds, I cannot fathom. The law on this matter is very clear. Any mobile worker visiting a site to make a delivery is classed as a contractor and is therefore entitled to access the same toilet facilities available to employees. This is covered under the HSE Workplace (Health, Safety, and Welfare) regulations of 1992 which can be downloaded for free from the HSE website. It is worth a read as I have often found that citing these particular regulations, chapter and verse at the available representative of any organisation reluctant to provide a visiting driver with relief, can miraculously and promptly change minds and quite literally open [toilet] doors.

I understand that I have something of a fixation regarding provisions for truck drivers but often these provisions are all that we have. We depend heavily upon what is provided for us for our physical well-being and personal dignity and too often our needs are given little thought or consideration. This includes the increasing tendency towards providing toilet cubicles reliant upon motion-sensitive lights. This concept works well during the day when each cubical is subject to constant use but when you are the only living soul in the building at night attempting to empty your bowels in the dark whilst frantically waving your hands around in the air above your head in order to reactivate the lights, you will understand the wisdom of a good old fashioned electrical switch.

Older drivers are stoical by nature and not inclined to complain. We have become too inured to being indifferently treated, to being taken for granted and cast aside when we become old, injured, or ill due to the nature of our work. To any young driver who is new to the game, this indifference towards the trucking fraternity comes as something of a shock and I have heard of many who survive little more than a year in the job that they have paid many thousands of pounds to become qualified in.

Attitudes towards drivers should and must change if haulage is to survive as a profession and those with the power to make that change should consider the fact that complacency and thoughtlessness may create a situation in a not too distant future where we run out of drivers long before automation makes our work obsolete.

LET IT SNOW

Everything an experienced driver needs to know regarding the way that his truck is handling can be felt through the seat of his pants. Seriously, I'm not kidding! If your tyres are cold and hard and the road icy, it can be felt in the form of an empty vibration that moves through the floor coupled with a lightness in the steering. This same lightness also indicates to the driver when he is about to aquaplane (a sensation which brings terror into the heart of any trucker). Whenever your load shifts your truck hits something, your tyres slip or you lose grip on the road, it will be noticed by your arse! (In more ways than one).

Strong winds can also be felt as well as seen, causing the trailer to swing from side to side and even lift off the axels, a sensation I have experienced on more than one occasion whilst towing a curtain-sided trailer along an exposed section of motorway.

The first time this occurred was less than two years into my trucking career on Christmas Eve 2000. Myself and a colleague in another vehicle had just made a delivery by curtain-sided wagon and drag (a large, rigid 18 tonne truck with a trailer) to a store in Exeter and we were in the process of making our winding way towards Bournemouth along the A35. It was an awfully stormy night and as we approached a particularly exposed section I watched in horror as the wheels on the nearside of my colleague's vehicle ahead of me, lifted off the tarmac and into the air. The entire combination of rigid and trailer balancing precariously on one side, continued forward for what felt like an eternity, though in reality was probably little more than a second, before crashing back onto the road, swerving a little, and continuing on its way.

Being less than five seconds behind both in distance and thought, I realised that the exact same thing was about to happen to me. It was to be the first (though not the last) truly terrifying moment of my career. The sensation of the lift, as though the hands of a giant had crept under the side of my vehicle and lifted it skywards. The angle, alarming, the steering, utterly ineffective. The descent to terra firma was equally unnerving as the steering wheel spun wildly out of my grip, wrenching my arms and almost breaking my thumbs. Thankfully, there was a large lay-by less than half a mile ahead where we were both able to pull over, take a deep breath and count ourselves lucky to be alive. How we managed to avoid a catastrophe that day is still a mystery to me.

There are many types of weather which are

hazardous to drivers. High winds being the most dangerous, snow being the most disruptive. Any strong gust of over 60mph is capable of bringing down a truck on an exposed road. At particular risk are double-deck trailers and curtain-sided trailers, double-decks because of their height and innate instability, and curtain-siders because not only does the wind build up beneath the trailer and quite literally lift the whole thing off its axels but because the wind also pushes itself into the trailer curtains causing them to billow inwards like the sail of a ship in a storm, pushing the trailer over.

High, exposed roads are obviously going to pose a greater threat to the driver on a windy day, along with high bridges (particularly those which cross the span of an estuary) and any Google or YouTube search into 'Truck Versus Wind' incidents will furnish you with a veritable plethora of horrifically graphic examples.

It also has to be said that driver error too can play its part. Driving too rapidly for the road conditions accounts for around 15% of fatalities in an average year. Driving too close to the vehicle in front reduces both visibility in poor conditions along with thinking and stopping time, occasionally resulting in disaster.

On a foggy night in November 2011, a multiple pile-up on the M5 northbound involving 34 vehicles (cars, trucks, and vans) occurred in thick fog when smoke from a bonfire and fireworks display being held in the grounds of an adjacent rugby club, drifted across the carriageway, further reducing driver visibility (though the fog was later found to be the primary cause). Seven were killed, fifty-one were injured. A total of 100 metres of road had to be resurfaced due to multiple vehicle fires or fuel damage and the carriageway was closed in both directions for two days. It was one of the worst ever incidents on a British motorway resulting from poor weather conditions and driver error. During that same year, a proposed increase to Motorway speed limits was being debated in both the media and parliament. This incident halted the debate immediately, never to be raised again.

Winter trucking is particularly miserable, and not just the driving aspect of the job. Loading and unloading in the freezing cold, howling wind, and driving rain can be unpleasant in the extreme. I can recall one incident when I was still a rookie and unused to curtain-sided trailers when I thought it would be a good idea to save time and open both sides of my trailer prior to being loaded on a windy day at Immingham Docks. I opened the nearside curtain closest to the dockside without issue, it was only as I released the front curtain pole and began to pull the offside curtain across that I realised my mistake. The wind now freely able to race straight across the centre of my trailer, whipped up the loose hanging curtains. Fearing that my curtain pole would swing out and cause injury to some unsuspecting forklift driver, I took hold of it. Within about half a second, I understood the error of my ways as the now billowing curtain began dragging me towards the edge of the dock. Fortunately, a nearby loader spotted my predicament and grabbed my waist. Without his foresight, I would have almost certainly found myself taking an unexpected plunge into the icy waters of the Humber.

In certain parts of the UK, snow, as well as fog and high winds, can be another serious hazard to truckers. Whilst much of the country would be sitting at home, curled up on the sofa enjoying a 'snow day' the average trucker would still be expected to keep the supermarket shelves stocked, driving in all but the worst of conditions.

Being a southerner and being out of the country during the 2009-2010 UK winter blizzard meant that my first significant experience of driving an LGV in deep snow came in 2016. A winter which also saw the UK being hit by several storms with wind speeds in excess of 70 mph. Driving in a blizzard is no less alarming for a truck driver than for a car driver. The swirling snow, just as disorientating, the loss of traction equally disturbing.

On this occasion, I was towing a fully laden double-deck trailer on a trunk run from Bristol to Newcastle-Under-Lyme at night. I left Bristol with barely a dusting of snow in our yard but by the time I arrived in Stoke-on-Trent, I could no longer see the position of the kerbstones along the road upon which I was travelling. By the time I reached the home stretch of my return journey, I was down to 15mph on the steeper sections of the M5, passing abandoned trucks and cars all along my route. A run which would normally take nine hours had taken close to fifteen and I was one of only a handful of our drivers who made it back to base without having to spend a night in a snowbound truck on the hard shoulder.

At the other end of the extreme weather scale, summer heatwaves can also cause problems for truckers. In the days before air conditioning and climate control was installed in all but a handful of vehicles as standard, I could often be found driving along the highways of the UK in little more than my underwear. Trucks have large windscreens and those windscreens allow a lot of heat to be drawn into the cab. More than once, I have been sitting in a truck which showed in excess 40 degrees Celsius on the thermometer. All that heat does not disperse easily and with the long, hot summer days we experience in the UK, it can be midnight before a driver on a night-out in summer can sleep comfortably in his truck.

Dehydration can also be an issue. I remember once making deliveries in Cornwall after closing time on one of the hottest days of the year. Each part of the load had to be carried manually (handballed) across a gravel courtyard and into an empty building. Being around 7 pm, there was no-one available to assist and the site was empty. I had run out of drinking water about an hour before arriving and by the time I finished the delivery, I was sticky, dripping with sweat, and could barely stand. I actually ended up knocking on the door of a stranger's house, begging for a glass of water. It took about two pints of blissfully cool liquid before I started feeling normal again.

Most experienced drivers check the road and weather conditions before they travel, it is always wise to be prepared for every eventuality that the British weather can throw at you. A long water-proof coat with a hood is essential along with a woolly hat in winter or a baseball cap in summer. Waterproof trousers may also be needed if you do a lot of manual loading (particularly when tow-ing curtain-sided trailers). In the UK, it is not un-known to experience four seasons in one day.

It is often said that there is no such thing as 'the wrong kind of weather, only the wrong kind of clothing' and that statement becomes all too apparent in this job. In winter, I can often be found wearing four or five layers of upper body cloth-ing (thermal vest, polo shirt, sweatshirt, fleece, waterproof coat) along with thermal long-johns and work trousers. This will be capped off with a woolly hat on my head and thick thermal socks in-side steel-toe-capped boots. In summer, I will be in steel-toe-capped shoes and rolled-up cotton work trousers with a polo shirt on top and my unruly hair contained beneath a baseball hat. Only experi-ence, many drenching's and many days covered in sweat and dust, teaches you the importance of wearing the right gear for the work required and there has to be nothing worse than spending the whole day in soaking wet clothing, steaming up the windows of your cab and wishing you had thought to bring a jacket.

THE FIRST CUT
IS THE DEEPEST

According to recent statistics, one in five UK road traffic accidents involves an LGV and for any newbie trucker, a serious accident can sometimes be enough to deter them from continuing in their career. It isn't just about the accidents which cause damage to vehicles and property, but also those which cause damage to the individuals involved. Many years ago, a good friend of mine came very close to hanging up his hi-vis for good when the corner of his truck struck a young woman who stepped off the kerb in a city centre without checking the road ahead of her. She lost her leg below the knee and my friend lost his job, his nerve, and his willingness to get back into an LGV for more than two years.

Due to the very nature of our work, drivers themselves suffer injury both on and off the road on a regular basis. These injuries will often be caused by poor manual handling techniques or slips, trips, and falls. A 2007 report stated that almost half of all non-driving-based trucking accidents occurred whilst loading and unloading and a further 15% occur whilst securing the load. When it came to falling from the vehicle, almost 40% involved incidents where the driver had fallen from the bed of the trailer and surprisingly only 8% from the tail-lift. Alarmingly, a further 8% actually fell from the roof!

On more than one occasion I have heard stories of drivers who have been seriously injured when they have stepped backwards off the edge of a tail-lift whilst making a delivery only to watch in abject horror as their load follows them over the side in hot pursuit.

One good friend and former colleague of mine caused permanent damage to his back whilst attempting to stow a particularly heavy and recalcitrant tail-lift. At the time, he had just finished making a delivery to an out of town shopping centre during the evening and as a consequence of his little fracas with the badly behaving tail-lift he soon found himself lying prone and in extreme pain on the floor of the loading bay where he remained for several hours before finally being discovered by shop staff who had been wondering why the truck was still parked outside.

For many years now, insurers have considered truck drivers to be the fourth most likely demographic to be injured or killed at work behind construction workers, farmers, and scaffolders or roofers. By contrast, firefighters, and military per-

LISA MARIE MELBOURNE

sonnel do not even feature within the top ten.

In my career of twenty-two years, I have known of, or have been personally connected, to dozens of drivers who have been killed or received life-changing injuries or permanent physiological damage whilst doing their jobs. Fortunately though, most of the time the injuries are minor. Bruises, cuts, and dents to one's pride are common. In the days when I was a store delivery driver and my work involved dragging wheeled cages or shrink-wrapped pallets of goods on and off the back of a trailer, I would often return home, undress for bed, and find cuts or bruises on my legs or arms and be left wondering how on earth they had got there in the first place!

Sometimes the casualties are not human at all. I have destroyed two phones as they slipped from my pocket and smashed into a million pieces on the tarmac and at least one pair of glasses when I opened my trailer door and a strong wind then wrenched it out of my hand resulting in the flying door handle hitting me in the face.

I have been fortunate enough to escape serious injury whilst working, though I have managed to break six bones in my lifetime simply by doing the most ordinary things, but I am digressing. My only major accident (so far) involved a rear-end shunt from a cement lorry.

Whilst travelling northbound on the A42 (a busy dual carriageway), I saw a broken-down car on the carriageway ahead of me. Knowing that this particular stretch of road provided only a very narrow hard shoulder, I began slowing and indicating to pull into the lane to my right. Sure enough, as I drew closer, the broken down car was positioned half on the tiny hard shoulder and half in the first live lane and there was barely enough room for an LGV to pass without entering the lane to the right. As my truck drew nearer and my speed decreased, I realised that no-one in the right-hand lane was going to give way and allow me to filter across. It was then that I glanced in my right-hand mirror to see a truck behind me in the right-hand lane, travelling at speed and whose driver was clearly not paying attention. To my horror, he then indicated to filter into the lane behind me. I was now down to about fifteen miles per hour and realised I had very few choices, in reality, only one choice. The truck was clearly about to rear-end my trailer and my only option was to brace and make my peace with God.

Fortunately, I had the presence of mind in the second before impact, to turn my wheel slightly to the right so that as the force of the impact, in true 'Newton's Cradle' fashion, pushed my rear-ended vehicle forward at terrific speed, I missed swiping the side of stationary broken down car by mere inches.

It was probably as well that I was on the ball that day because I later discovered that the occupant of the car was, at that moment, minus her seat belt and attempting the exit the vehicle through the passenger side door.

On that occasion, everyone walked away from the incident with little more than cuts, bruises, shock, and a little whiplash but it could so easily have resulted in catastrophe.

My trailer was a write-off, as no doubt, was the cement truck and all because someone allowed their attention to be diverted from the road for a few seconds, but that is all it takes. That is the fine line that truckers walk along every day, the fine line between life and death.

Of course, every driver knows this, but if any one of us were to stop and think about this too much or for too long, we would never leave the house.

Most incidents experienced by drivers are usually humiliating, terrifying, or expensive (sometimes all of these things). These can include, but are not limited to:

Exiting the cab without putting on the hand-brake.

Releasing the trailer brake without having ensured that the handbrake in the tractor unit was engaged and watching in horror as your unit and trailer roll down the hill without you.

Pulling away from a loading bay when your trailer is still being loaded and scaring the hell out of the warehouse staff who may well still be working in the back of your trailer.

Moving your tractor unit out from under your

trailer without first lowering the trailer legs so that your trailer hits the floor rather unceremoniously.

Driving off without first properly securing your doors or some part of your load.

Setting the height of your tractor unit too low when coupling to a trailer and slamming the rear of your cab into the front of your trailer.

Any one of these rookie mistakes can prove to be costly or dangerous in the extreme. They will all result in disciplinary action, and some would result in summary dismissal. Almost all drivers will have at some point in their career committed, or very nearly committed, at least one of these mistakes.

Certainly, my most humiliating error ever occurred in the centre of Bath on a fine summer morning in 1999.

I was delivering to a store in a rigid 18-tonne vehicle using a roadside loading bay situated outside the front of the shop. Unbeknownst to me, Bath has these things called 'cellar lights' inserted into the pavements outside of many of its town centre stores. These are little blocks of glass within a metal frame set into the ground which give light to the cellars below and which extend out and away from the shops.

The day before, some work had been carried out on the pavement in front of the store I was delivering to and sand had been scattered across the slabs, completely obscuring the cellar lights from view. On my approach to the loading area (which was little better than a compact parking spot on the side of the road), I noticed that two cars had parked at either end, shortening the space available to me. Being that I was in a large rigid vehicle, I took a steeper than usual angle into the bay and mounted the pavement intending to then steer out of the bay so that my vehicle would drop down off the kerb close to the edge of the pavement and in a nice, neat, straight line.

Unaware that I had just driven eighteen tonnes of truck over a slab of unsupported metal and glass, I was somewhat surprised to hear an ominous cracking sound coming from below and watched in horror as the whole of the offside front of my truck dropped away and slid towards the front of the shop window. It finally came to rest, perched at an alarming angle, sitting on the front axle with one wheel hanging precariously in mid-air over a large hole. To add insult to injury, the impact burst a mains water pipe beneath me and flooded several cellars that day. I had to wait three hours for a towing vehicle to arrive and winch me to safety during which time the whole incident was being enthusiastically photographed by several locals and a gaggle of Japanese tourists.

Until the day that I left that company, some years later, I never lived it down and it was at least three months following that incident before my company allowed me to make deliveries in Bath again!

DEATH COMES KNOCKING

As I have previously mentioned, truckers are the fourth most likely demographic of employees to suffer death or injury at work, equating to an average of around twenty deaths per year on UK roads. This does not include the deaths of lorry drivers which take place in depots and warehouses, on the exhausting commute home, or as a result of a health condition created or exacerbated by this particular line of work. These are the hidden statistics of trucker deaths and they far exceed the often more well-reported and spectacular RTA's involving LGV's. In fact, barely a year goes by when I do not hear tell of the death of an individual I am tenuously connected to through colleagues or the various companies that I, or they, have worked for or delivered to.

Many of the larger haulage firms or trade unions now offer their staff excellent accident and life insurance packages as a result of these statistics. On a personal note, I am insured up to the eyeballs. In twenty years in this industry, I have worked for at least half a dozen companies that have experienced the death of a driver employee, either on the site itself or due to an RTA.

I can recall two particularly horrific incidents where drivers were crushed to death, either by their own vehicles or that of another driver. The first of which came about when the driver coupled his trailer to his tractor unit without engaging the tractor unit handbrake inside the cab. When the trailer brake was then released, the combination of unit and trailer began to move forward down the slope. The driver, panicking, tried to re-enter the cab to engage the tractor unit handbrake and stop the vehicle. Unfortunately, this meant that he had to run in front of the moving truck in order to enter through the passenger side and the vehicle struck him, the full weight of it crushing him against the gatepost whereupon it finally came to rest.

Of course, had he been thinking more clearly, he could simply have re-engaged the trailer brake as soon as the vehicle began moving, though there can be no doubt that this little nugget of hindsight would be of no consolation whatsoever to his family.

The second incident I can recall occurred when a driver acting as a banksman (someone who helps another driver reverse by standing to the rear of his vehicle and making sure he doesn't hit anything) was driven into and crushed by the vehicle of his friend and colleague. Quite how this came about, I am unsure though you can be certain that one, or both, of these individuals, was somehow distracted from the task at hand resulting in the death of one and permanent emotional scarring of the other.

Driver fatigue is often at the root of many of these types of fatalities regardless of when, where, or how they occur, and whilst there are many trades, vocations, and occupations that typically work longer hours, many of those would do so predominantly during daylight hours and the work itself would not involve operating heavy and dangerous machinery for the majority of that time. There is a world of difference between undertaking ten hours of clerical work and undertaking ten hours of night-time driving in control of a potential murder machine.

Then there is of course the toll that night-time working takes upon your long-term health. Sleeping during the day and working at night reduces the amount of vitamin D the body absorbs from sunlight. This can increase the risk of cancer, heart disease, and depression. Lack of light also depresses the body's production of Melatonin, a hormone produced by the pineal gland, essential for deep, restful sleep, without which the body does not repair itself fully between sleep cycles resulting in insomnia and other sleep disorders. Long working hours and irregular shift patterns can also create this effect and if there is one thing in this world that no-one should be doing whilst tired, it is driving 44 tonnes of truck.

Then there are, of course, other issues which can further affect a driver's health and accelerate his demise. Chief amongst these is obesity and all that comes with it. This can lead to diabetes, high blood pressure, and heart failure, and once again changes to the hormone structure and metabolism caused by fatigue are at the root of all this. Poor diet, of course, does not help and the temptation to snack on sugary foods when tired further exacerbates the problem by adding to already ample hips and expanding waistlines. (My own proportions being no exception here).

Exercise (or lack thereof) is also an issue. Many drivers find themselves exhausted at the end of a full working day, so an evening run or a visit to the gym is often the last thing on their minds. Free time is also an issue when working long hours and for most drivers, if they wish to maintain anything resembling a home or social life, an evening with their family or friends will always take preference over an hour or two of exercise. This lack of adherence to a healthy lifestyle, coupled with a fairly sedentary occupation will cause weight gain and other complications, further shortening the life of the average trucker.

Irregular mealtimes and unhealthy eating habits are also a contributing factor with up to 84% of UK truckers being classed as obese. Although I was unable to find statistics stating the life expectancy of truck drivers in the UK, in the

USA it is alarmingly low at the tender age of 61. I don't imagine that the UK fares much better although we are far more heavily regulated with regards to standards of training and limits on maximum working hours.

For more information on how truck driving directly affects health and life expectancy, I would recommend the HSE's Occupational Health and Extended Working Lives in the Transport Sector Research Report (RR1104). It certainly makes for sober reading.

For those of us who engage in manual labour as part of our working day, the outlook is far brighter. Delivering heavy cages or pallets laden with shrink-wrapped goods for retail stores makes for excellent daily exercise. This manner of work is often undertaken by younger, fitter drivers. It is tough and demanding, often involving many drops per day (the smaller the vehicle, the greater the number of deliveries). Usually, this is predominantly day work, stressful, and time-critical. It involves offloading in front of, or at the rear of, shops using a tail-lift with a sack-truck, wheeled cages, or a pallet truck.

As with all types of trucking work (and there are many kinds), it is very much a case of 'horses for courses'. Some drivers love the hard manual work and others prefer the more sedentary nature of long-distance trunking but they are both fraught with risk. During the daytime the traffic is more numerous, increasing the likelihood of accidents. If your work is time-critical, you are more likely to cut corners and take risks thereby increasing your chances of injury.

Many drivers begin their careers making manual deliveries and over time, progress inevitably towards a more stately way of working.

I spent at least the first fifteen years of my trucking life manually offloading (also known as 'handballing') goods. At one time, I worked for a large industrial baker and although the work involved long-distance trunking from bakery to warehouse, we had to unload our own trailers. This involved manhandling trays of bread using a pulling bar, dragging each one along the deck of the trailer to the rear doors, where it was collected by the fork-lift truck and taken to where it was needed within the warehouse. Each stack consisted of around fifteen trays, was twice my body weight, and around six feet in height. At either end of this exhausting day, I would cycle ten miles to work and ten miles home again over the old Severn Bridge, often at night and in all but the harshest and stormiest of weather. In those days I was as fit as a flea and had arms that a Russian shot-putter would envy but as my grandmother would say 'age does not come alone' and eventually it (along with several nasty injuries) caught up with me.

The nature of our work also releases a driver from many of the expected social 'norms', which for those without a high degree of self-discipline, can result in over-indulgence and an unerring ten-

dency towards unhealthy or antisocial habits.
These can include:

Talking to yourself (because there is no-one else to talk to).
Overeating (because there is no-one to tell you not to).
Eating too rapidly (because there is no-one to disapprove of you).
Farting and belching very loudly (because there is no-one to glare at you).
Smoking or vaping (because who is around to care)?

There can be no doubt that driving a truck and all that goes with it affects directly or indirectly the general health, well-being, and life expectancy of the driver.

A recent survey by the union, Unite, suggested that 29% of truck drivers surveyed had at least once in their career, fallen asleep at the wheel. Personally, I feel that is a conservative estimate and that the true number is far greater. Obviously, falling asleep at the wheel is not conducive to longevity, for the driver or anyone else in the vicinity for that matter, and accidental death and injury aside, many leave this industry long before retirement age due to sickness, stress, incapacity, or infirmity.

Some drivers with skills in other areas find themselves progressing from trucking to driver training or into management but the call of the open road is loud and persistent and I have known of several who have eventually returned to trucking life after many years away from the 'coal face' simply because they miss the sense of freedom that work engenders.

LIVING IN A BOX

So, those of you who have never driven a truck, or been inside one for that matter, may be wondering what it is like to make one your home for a week or more, so I shall do my best to explain.

Doing 'nights out' sleeping in your vehicle during your working week is known as 'Tramping', a title probably given to this type of work to describe what your life will become (like that of a tramp). Well, that's my theory anyway!

It is not easy to live in a space approximately 8ft wide, 8ft deep, and between 6ft and 8ft high (and that's if you are fortunate enough to have a high cab truck).

Your bed could best be described as basic, the mattress is of the fabric-covered foam variety and is normally between 2ft 6 inches and 3ft 6 inches wide, though they are often slightly longer than that of a standard mattress. Some are extremely comfortable though others are little more than a thin padded covering over an unforgiving base, it really depends upon whether or not you are driving a low or high-spec vehicle and some manufacturers pay more attention to driver comfort than others. (I'm not naming any names here, but you know who you are!)

Other than your bunk (and if you are doing nights out in your vehicle, a sleeping bunk is required by law) your only other guaranteed comfort is a set of wrap-around curtains and a night heater. The latter should only be used when your vehicle is stationary. They are powered using the fuel in your diesel tank and are not as silent as one would hope, though as technology has developed, they have become significantly quieter with the passing years compared to how they were when I first started.

Other than storage lockers of varying sizes and capacities, your truck may also be fitted with other 'luxuries' including alarm clock, sunroof, fridge, 12v and 24v charging points, a radio and well...... that's about it, though there is a seemingly endless number of gadgets that drivers can buy in order to 'pimp up their rides'. These include fridges, kettles, food warmers, ovens, sandwich toasters, microwaves, TV's, CB radios (yes, some drivers still use them) truck sat-navs, extra light bars with which to blind oncoming drivers, fancy paint jobs, deafening air horns and shiny wheel trims. Some of these non-standard items are usually purchased by owner-drivers rather than those who use a company-owned vehicle, which could be given to another trucker at a moment's notice.

So, as you can see, a truck really can become home from home, albeit a very cramped and compact one. Other essentials for truckers would include comfortable bedding, night-wear (this is usually leisurewear, since no-one wants to see a trucker queuing for the showers in slippers, P.J's, and a dressing gown) a toilet bucket (for ladies) loo roll, and wet wipes, a large water container and washing up bowl, towels, cab shoes (usually flip-flops) cleaning equipment and bin liners.

As previously mentioned, truck parking doesn't come cheap though in recent times with the advent of smartphones, many new Apps (such as Intruck) have been developed to make finding and paying for a suitable parking spot a much more straightforward experience. For the drivers whose employers have opened accounts with companies such as SNAP, the hassle of making a payment in cash for parking and then filing for reimbursement through expenses has been completely eliminated. All the driver has to do is find the right location according to his need and reserve his place, his employer will then be invoiced directly. Often these apps will provide the driver with crucial information such as parking capacity, available spaces, facilities provided, and full contact details.

When looking for a suitable night out location, drivers usually hope for a quiet area, not too bright or too dark and gloomy, on clean level ground (sleeping on a slope is uncomfortable in the extreme) away from entrances and exits and hopefully, nowhere near a noisy refrigerated lorry.

Obviously, if paying for a service area or truck-stop one would often expect showering facilities and a meal voucher to be included within the parking fee. If sleeping in a layby, ablutions are often performed in the rear of the trailer in the form of a strip wash, this is why night-out drivers carry a large water container though I know of some drivers who have been able to pay to use the facilities of a local gym, swimming pool or leisure centre. Any other type of ablutions are usually undertaken in the toilet of the nearest service station or whatever facilities are available at the time unless of course, you are the kind of driver for which the title of 'tramper' is particularly apt.

Tramping work is not for everyone and obviously for some with dependents, could prove to be completely impractical but it is the ultimate test of a driver's mettle since you will be expected to calmly and efficiently solve any problems you encounter. Isolation too can be an issue since you will often find that unless you have good friends or family who do not mind if you call them up and use them as a sounding board for all your woes, you can go for many days with little conversation or interaction, though other drivers are often more than willing to offer help and advice to newbies and rookies so getting into conversation with the 'old hands' if overnighting in a lorry park can be both rewarding and entertaining.

So once you are parked up for the night, what should you expect? Well firstly, you should ensure that you have paid to park. In days gone by a driver would look for a payment cabin with a ticket attendant. These days, you will probably be expected to pay at the 24-hour shop (if using a service station) or the main café or reception (if using a truck-stop) that's if you have not pre-booked using one of the aforementioned apps.

It is usually better to shower in the evening since you will be less rushed and the queues will be fewer, though unfortunately, the facilities are more likely to be fairly well used by then and not quite as clean.

Unless you provide all your own food, you can expect nourishment standards to vary wildly in price, quality and content and therefore, it is wise to bring with you the food which you will enjoy, rather than having to rely upon what is available wherever you are.

Many European truckers bring gas stoves with them though it is extremely unwise to use these inside the cab, in fact, many truck stops and service stations expressly prohibit their use, as do many UK haulage firms. Electrical appliances are slower but safer and can be used inside the vehicle without the likelihood of setting your truck on fire!

In winter your truck will cool rapidly once you are parked up so one of your first jobs before you pay for parking and go for a shower, should be to turn on your cab heater. There is nothing worse than coming back to your truck and having to undress for bed in freezing temperatures.

In the summer, you will be faced with the opposite problem. If you are able to park in the shade or without the sun on the windscreen, you should do so. It may also seem counter-intuitive but it is usually a good idea to draw the curtains or pull down the blinds and open the sun roof (if you have one). Sleeping in a stifling hot truck can be very unpleasant but a clip-on fan plugged into the 24-volt system (which is sometimes permanently live) can really help. You may also find a 'Hella' plug socket which tends to stay pugged in more reliably whilst on the move, though you usually have to buy an adaptor for this.

You may find that your dashboard has many dials, levers and buttons which are unfamiliar and not found in your average car. These can include a button for the forward-facing camera, the diff-lock, the lift axel and one for making slow manoeuvres or hill starts, a lever for the exhaust brake and an abundance of buttons for adjusting the suspension on the rear of the tractor unit.

Then there are all the light buttons. The usual headlights and fog lights but also an external inspection light at the rear of the cab and various internal floodlights, driving lights and reading lights along with a dimmer switch for the instrument panel (great when you are driving at night).

The instrument panel itself could rival that of the starship enterprise with vehicle diagnostics, built-in GPS systems and Bluetooth controls.

You should also be aware that there are many different kinds of sleeping bunks. The usual type is situated behind the seats but occasionally you will come across double bunks, the second bunk being attached to the rear wall of the cab which then folds down. This dramatically reduces the head room of the bunk below and is rarely used, except by drivers who double-man as a team. This is where you have two drivers sharing duties, meaning that the maximum daily shift can be extended for up to 20 hours though each driver must follow and precede that with a minimum of 9 hours of rest. Double manning and double-bunking is usually only undertaken by those covering extremely long distances. It is worth noting that the 9-hour daily rest cannot be taken by the non-driving party whilst the vehicle is moving since there are no seatbelts on a bunk.

Double bunks are sometimes necessary but they are awkward and not liked or trusted by all drivers. I have heard more than one tale of a top bunk breaking and nearly crushing the sleeping driver below.

There is another kind of bunk that can sometimes be found on rigid vehicles and is a type known as a sleeper pod but which I like to refer to as 'The Coffin'.

These are little extensions positioned on the roof of the cab and are accessed through a trap door above the passenger seat. The proportions are claustrophobic to put it politely and I have to confess that even in the days when I was a svelte 29-year old I found it a struggle to crawl, roll, squirm and shimmy into the space. Sitting up once inside was awkward, escape in an emergency situation, all but impossible. The nickname is apt, should your stationary vehicle catch fire, your only form of egress would literally be a headlong dive through the tiny window provided at one end.

SLAVE TO THE SAT-NAV

Advances in modern technology have revolutionised trucking in recent years. When I first passed my LGV test in 1998, lorry drivers were still very heavily relying upon paper maps with which to navigate the UK highways and byways. Each driver would carry, as part of their essential daily kit, a trucker's atlas at the very least. This is a large, detailed road atlas, displaying the locations of all the low bridges, width, length and weight restrictions along all the major and minor roads in the country (with the exception of small residential streets and country lanes).

Supplementing this considerably weighty tome, the driver would additionally carry any local maps and A-Z's that he may require, along with any necessary hand-drawn maps showing him how to get to delivery and collection points along his route.

As you can imagine, all of this paper would amount to considerable weight and bulk, and would all be stuffed into the driver's rucksack or hold-all along with his gloves, tachograph waxed paper disks (prior to the introduction of digital tachograph cards in 2006) his lunch, water, music tapes, torch, wallet and anything else he considered important enough to carry around with him.

The popularity and availability of the Sat Nav in the early 2000s, changed all of this and no doubt many drivers with heavy bags and sciatica, breathed a great sigh of relief. At first, the developers did not consider the needs of truckers and the first popular Sat Nav's available in the UK did not show any of the things which truckers need to know (such as the locations of low bridges). This resulted in an increase of bridge strikes (where a driver attempts to squeeze his unit and trailer beneath a bridge far too low for his vehicle) and an increase in incidents of drivers becoming stuck in roads which were impassible for LGV's.

This is because, unless you have a Truckers' Sat Nav, it will always direct the driver along the shortest or quickest route regardless of the road width or any inconveniently placed 13ft high railway bridge.

There have even been reports of drivers being directed by their Sat Nav through rivers, along railway lines, down cycle paths and even over the edges of cliff tops or harbour walls.

There were also several rather well-known incidents of truckers (usually newbies or European drivers) who were unaware of the particularly British quirk of having more than one town with the same (or similar) name. These can often be located many, many miles apart from each other such as:

Stamford Bridge, London and Stamford Bridge, East Yorkshire

St Ives, Cornwall and St Ives, Cambridgeshire

Ripley, North Yorkshire and Ripley, Surrey

I found one story where a Syrian trucker drove his 32-tonne truck to Gibraltar Point in Lincolnshire when he was actually supposed to be making a delivery to the Island of Gibraltar, a detour of more than 1,600 miles. Several years ago, I remember reading about a Polish driver who was supposed to make a delivery to Newcastle-Upon-Tyne and ended up in Newcastle-Under-Lyme instead.

I too have been the victim of a Sat Nav error whilst working as a trade-plater, hitch-hiking all the way through Cumbria to a hamlet close to the town of Cockermouth when I should have been collecting from an industrial estate of the same name just outside of Carlisle.

These are but a few of the horrors which await the unsuspecting driver without a postcode or enough of the relevant information on their paperwork and really goes to prove that if a Sat Nav is to be used, a heavy dollop of common sense needs also to be applied alongside it.

According to the RAC, errors relating to Sat

Nav use, cause close to £200,000,000 worth of damage every year, some of that would include some fairly spectacular mistakes on the part of the trucking fraternity. It is a sad reflection upon both truck and bus drivers that there are an average of five bridge strikes every day in the UK and some of these would have been indirectly caused by the use of the wrong kind of Sat Nav.

I cannot overstate the importance of 'knowing your route' and if a Sat Nav is to be used, it should be one which is designed for trucks. These systems allow the driver to enter his vehicle's weight, height, width and length into the settings. The Sat Nav will then find the best and safest route according to his specifications, ensuring that the driver avoids bridges which are too low and roads which are too narrow or weight restricted. In addition, the Sat Nav may also inform the driver of traffic congestion ahead, speed restrictions, truck stops, service areas and transport cafes along his route.

However, even a Truckers' Sat Nav can cause difficulties of its own. I have worked for more than one company which does not allow its drivers to use a Sat Nav and instead provides each driver with a detailed book of paper maps showing how to get to each delivery point. The reason for this is not because the transport manager is a technophobe but simply because it is believed that drivers cannot be trusted to engage their common sense. In some cases, it is simply believed that the device itself causes a distraction to the driver, or if attached to the windscreen, an obstruction to his view.

Personally, I disagree. In a modern truck with all the training given to drivers nowadays, the vast majority of us are quite capable of following a Truck Sat Nav without being fatally distracted from the task at hand. After all, we already have so many dashboard lights and dials to which we must pay attention along with the position of our vehicle behind us and the conditions of the road ahead of us, so the lights and noises of a Truck Sat Nav are hardly going to tip us over the edge into a state of distraction.

Many truck manufactures are beginning to catch on to the need for reliable and safe navigation and in recent years have begun installing Sat Nav's into their higher-end vehicles as standard, though many drivers still prefer to use their own familiar devices with places of interest, favourite routes and delivery points already saved in the settings.

The devices themselves have come a long way in recent years. When they first became available, the price could be compared to a fortnight's wage for a trucker but the cost since then has reduced considerably. A quick Amazon search listed several 'all singing, all dancing' devices with a 7 or 8-inch display for less than £200 which include a dash-cam, voice-activated dialling, Wi-Fi and various other features.

If the cost is still a little eye-watering there are several free truckers navigating apps on the market such as Road Lords which will help you to navigate the UK roads safely, avoiding low bridges and other restrictions, providing live traffic updates and information along with places of interest to drivers. It is an interactive app so the drivers themselves can add to the usefulness of the app by submitting additional information such as thefts in the area, accidents and mobile speed cameras or make requests for assistance from other drivers using the app. All a far cry from my days as a driver in the early 2000's when I was expected to find my way around the country using a combination of maps, wits and a whole lot of luck.

For many new truckers, it is something akin to their worst nightmare to find themselves stuck halfway down a road that turns out to be unpassable for LGV's or to take a wrong turning and find themselves faced with a low bridge and no-where to turn around. It is fair to say that I would be lying if I pretended that an incident such as this had never happened to me. It should also be said that the only thing worse than having no map, is having an inaccurate map.

I recall one occasion where I was given a printed map from an online navigation program that pinpointed my delivery location and highlighted the route I should take, only to find upon arrival in the area that the highlighted route was impassable for LGV's. The result of this debacle was that I had to reverse back along the winding, single-track country lane, in which I found myself, for approximately a quarter of a mile, at night and in the driving rain, before being able to turn my vehicle around on a main road and find a more appropriate route. Had I been an inexperienced driver, this incident would have terrified me.

A 44-tonne truck is no small thing to man-oeuvre and 'big truck, small space' anxiety is common amongst newbies. When I first started I often found myself drinking far less water than I normally would, simply due to the fear of needing to stop and park up in a less than desirable 'smaller than I could handle' parking bay, so that I could answer a call of nature.

Even with a reliable truck Sat-Nav, additional hand-drawn maps are always helpful, particularly when they have been drawn by the drivers themselves. It is the habit of planners, architects and site designers to make things as difficult for the trucker as possible by creating loading and unloading points which are not signposted, difficult to use or reverse onto and peppered with obstructions and unexpected hazards. When it comes to safe trucking, information is king and if that information comes first hand from another lorry driver, it can usually be trusted. If the navigational information has been provided by any other source, it should be taken only with a heavy dose of caution.

SAY HELLO, WAVE GOODBYE

As I have previously alluded to, the life of a trucker can be a very lonely one. This is particularly true for trampers and night trunkers. Most haulage companies run a skeleton staff throughout the night, signing drivers in and handing over paperwork and keys. Much of the admin is undertaken during office hours so what can be a busy site during the day can be almost deserted by the evening. Night drivers often find their circle of communication shrinking due to the fact that they are at work whilst most of their more conventional peers are at home in their beds. Their road ahead may be quieter but their life is surely more empty for it.

For trampers, their world is their truck. They eat in it, sleep in it, relax and watch TV in it so it often becomes their own little haven of tranquillity. Those they meet and speak to whilst making deliveries may be the only individuals they will have the chance to communicate with face to face, throughout the entirety of their working week.

Divorce and relationship break-up rates are, as you would expect, disproportionately high amongst lorry drivers. Much is expected of the spouse of a trucker who may not see his own front door from one weekend to the next. Even for those who do return to base every night, the long and unsociable hours mean that drivers miss out on family life, the responsibility of which often falls entirely upon the shoulders of their partner.

Even for the unattached, life is still tough and unless you share your home with friends or family members, your communication circle will shrink to minuscule proportions and your social life may disappear altogether. Recent statistics suggest that the truck driver suicide rate could be as much as 20% above the national average with loneliness and isolation cited as the root cause. There would certainly be other factors hidden within these statistics such as depression caused by insomnia or melatonin and vitamin imbalances due to an unhealthy diet or nighttime and irregular working schedules but certainly, isolation does not help.

It takes a certain kind of individual to be a trucker and not everyone handles it well. Many of today's school leavers would generally find that the life of a lorry driver would fall very far short of their future goals and expectations but for some, this world is a perfect fit. Trucking suits well those who like their lives to be a little less ordinary, those who are considered unconventional and those who find that they need their own space and freedom to feel at ease. The ideal trucker would be one who enjoys the company of others but does not crave it, one who chooses friends carefully and keeps his own council, not seeking the approval of others.

Truckers are often perceived as loners and of course, there is some truth in that but they can also be some of the most caring and compassionate people you will ever meet. A trucker is a problem solver, he (or she) is the person you want to have by your side in a crisis. When incidents occur on the road, it is often the trucker with his superior training and unflappable nature who will direct the traffic, administer first aid or call the emergency services.

However because of our tenuous connections to our depots (I am actually in the office of our site for less than 30 minutes each day) we rarely make meaningful connections to our work colleagues or fellow drivers. I am embarrassed to confess that although I have worked at my current depot for almost three years, I know the names of only a small number of the people I work with, a social blind spot common amongst drivers.

Since I am only one of three female lorry drivers amongst a compliment of over one hundred, my name is well known but as a rule, visiting truckers are often referred to as "Drive" whilst on-site (as though it is all we are or all we ever do)!

We are the anonymous, the underappreciated, the unloved backbone of this country's economy and to many, we are seen as little more than a necessary evil. We drive hundreds of miles to deliver to a site and often receive, in return, little more than a nod of acknowledgement as we hand over our paperwork.

However, I have made several lifelong friends through my work, and though I rely heavily upon technology to keep in touch with those I care about, it is still possible to maintain strong bonds of love and friendship.

The road is long and lonely but Bluetooth and voice-activated dialling systems have become the saviour of many a long-distance relationship. Those who drive at night or travel many miles between delivery points use these new forms of technology to keep in touch with their friends and loved ones and whilst it could be considered a distraction, it can also go a long way towards staving off boredom and fatigue.

For many truckers, there is a world of difference between being alone and being lonely. The first can be liberating, the other can be soul-destroying but spending so much of your working life away from family, friends and one's own home can affect everyday life in unexpected ways. For the unattached driver who tramps and returns home only at weekends, their spare time is often filled with mundane tasks in preparation for the week ahead with little effort given and little time taken towards socialising or visiting family. The cumulative effect of this over several years can result in a rapidly dwindling social circle, the driver becoming trapped in a world of one. Him or herself!

For those with children and spouses at home, the ongoing weekly separation means that the driver will miss key moments in the life of his or her children, will not be present in times of crisis and be unavailable when help and support is required.

For most people working 'normal' hours in a nine to five type of environment, if a family emergency arises, they can simply leave and go home to handle it. For a truck driver, this is not an option since they may be many miles from home when a situation arises that requires their immediate attention.

Then there is the issue of making appointments. How does a driver who lives alone and works away all week get anything handled? How does he get the car serviced, see a doctor, go to the bank or get a broken tooth filled when all the organisations which provide such services are open Monday to Friday only? One answer, of course, is to take a day off and possibly lose pay since popping out to the dentist on one's lunch break is not usually an option. The other answer is simply not to bother. So many drivers neglect their own health and welfare as attending to it diligently is simply too much trouble.

Many of us, being the age that we are, just get on with it. If we bother to handle our health at all, we simply try to fix the issues ourselves either with supplements or with over-the-counter medicines. We tend not to share our problems which can lead to further difficulties since a driver is alone for much of the working day and without others to talk to, pressure can build up and push us over the edge somewhat.

Drivers are well known for their capacity to moan and grumble sometimes, but in truth, it is because we often have no one with which to air our views, put the world to rights or discuss our day.

Any small problem or niggle can be blown up out of all proportion by the trucker with too much time to think and not enough opportunity to talk.

On the flip side of this situation though, trucking can fuel the creative juices of those inclined towards the arts. The job allows an individual time to reflect, to dream and imagine. I have formed the structure of dozens of books, whole volumes of poetry and solved myriad of seemingly imponderable problems whilst sat at the wheel of a lorry. But free time is a double-edged sword. For the busy mind it is a blessing but for the worrier, a curse.

A person can easily wind themselves up into quite a pickle without friends or family around to talk them down. Anger takes longer to disperse and anxiety can linger for days when you are unable to solve that which is troubling you and truckers are not the kind of men or women that you are likely to find reclining in the therapist's chair.

So the next time a truck driver starts bending your ear, just keep in mind that you may very well be the only person he will get to speak with today, buy him a coffee, tell him a joke and do something to make him (or her) smile. Laughter makes the world a brighter place and a trucker's life is made all the better for it.

FULLY LOADED

Safe loading and strapping of cargo is something all new drivers struggle with. When I first started driving 7.5-tonne trucks in 1995 training was scant, to say the least, and I'm ashamed to say that an unhealthy degree of trial and error went into learning how best to load my cargo and secure it effectively.

These days, most haulage firms train all their new and experienced drivers in the various methods of safely loading and securing a wide variety of different types of cargo in an effort to reduce risk, damage and wastage.

During 2013 alone the DVSA issued over 2,000 prohibition notices to vehicles that presented a road safety risk because of their load security (or lack thereof). A prohibition notice can result in the detainment of the vehicle or impoundment and prosecution of the driver and employer. In March 2015 they issued a document on their website entitled 'Load Securing: Vehicle Operator Guide' which has been updated several times since. I would recommend it as good bedtime reading for all those involved in the transportation of goods by road.

There are many ways in which to safely load and strap cargo in accordance with the type of goods being transported and the type of vehicle being used but there are only a few basic golden rules, which are as follows.

Make sure you are using the right vehicle for the job, know the weight of the load and the carrying capacity of the vehicle you are using.

Avoid using curtain-sided vehicles for goods in wheeled cages, unless the cages have brakes and the vehicle has been specially designed to carry them.

Make sure you have an adequate number of load restraints, check they are undamaged and of the right kind for the type of cargo you will be transporting.

Ensure that all loose items are secured into their cages or shrink-wrapped onto their pallets.

Before loading your cargo, make sure that each item is not too heavy, too tall or likely to topple over.

Distribute the weight as evenly as possible.

Do not leave gaps between items, particularly front to back. Gaps represent an opportunity for your load to move.

Use all straps or load restraining bars provided. This should be a minimum of one strap or bar for every three or four rows, sometimes more than that, depending on the type of cargo being transported and the type of vehicle being used.

Always strap or bar the last row nearest the doors of your trailer.

Obviously, there is more to it than this, but follow these basic rules and you will not go too far wrong. I have learned by bitter experience that there is a right and a wrong way to restrain a load but you do not need to be a physics genius to understand what will happen to your cargo in an emergency braking situation, the results of which are often not pretty. Employers are not generally impressed by goods that arrive damaged as a result of poor loading and restraining. At best you will have one hell of a clean-up job on your hands and at worst you could cause death or injury to yourself or others either on the road or in the depot where the unloading of your cargo will take place.

I can recall one particularly memorable incident which occurred whilst working for a small, local paint producer near Bristol. I was contracted that week to deliver to Cornwall and Devon over the span of two days in an eighteen-tonne truck. I arrived at my first drop and opened the back doors to find the inside of the truck looking like an explosion in a yoghurt factory. There was white emulsion paint everywhere, all over the floor, the walls and many of the other cans of paint. All of this from one single 15-litre tub which had escaped the restraint of the cage it was being transported in due to a simple broken latch. It had proceeded to have itself a jolly old time, rolling around in the back of my wagon all the way to Cornwall. The clean-up operation took hours and I made barely half of my deliveries but I learned a valuable lesson that day.

Always check all of the restraints of your cargo and if someone else has loaded it, check and check again. As soon as you leave your depot, you are responsible if anything goes wrong. The buck always stops with the driver, no one else.

Everything that is transported in the back of a truck must be secured or it will move. Even pallet trucks, sack trucks, tail-lift safety bars and load restraining bars should be made safe so that they cannot shift in transit and cause damage to goods or to the inside of the trailer.

If you have ever been a passenger in a car whilst overtaking a truck, you will notice that the trailer itself bends and flexes as it travels along the road. This movement also affects the stability of the cargo and can cause restraints to loosen. This is why a drivers' straps must be tight and why his cargo should be without gaps between pallets.

An unrestrained load can kill, anything which can slide (such as sheet steel) is particularly dangerous and on a recent CPC course we were all treated to a truly horrific YouTube clip of a driver who had failed to secure the scaffolding he was carrying. When the vehicle in front of him braked to avoid a collision the scaffolding driver followed suit but his cargo did not. This resulted in a dozen large, heavy metal poles, breaking through the bulkhead of his trailer and into the rear of his cab, killing him instantly.

During this same CPC course (I swear that the trainer had a sadistic streak) we were shown another clip of what can happen to bottles of unrestrained pressurised gas in a road traffic incident. Let's just say that none of us left that room with the idea of breaking out the BBQ at the weekend.

Some loads are always going to be easier to handle than others. Most palletised goods give little trouble but anything shrink-wrapped should be regarded with suspicion. The worst culprits are those which contain many loose items (such as boxes and bottles) of varying shapes and sizes. These are extremely difficult to stack, even by those with a keen love of Jenga or Tetrus, and even harder to wrap or strap securely. They also have a tendency to lean or topple over in transit in a most inconvenient fashion.

I used to make regular deliveries to a high street retailer (they shall remain anonymous) whose goods were almost always stacked and wrapped in this manner. Usually, the stacking and wrapping were good but occasionally, whoever was in charge of this particular task would have an 'off' day and you would arrive at the store to find almost every pallet leaning drunkenly into its neighbour, the whole wagon load resembling a rugby team on a pub crawl.

This particular store had many branches across the country, one of which provided the driver with a particularly tricky loading bay with what must have been a one in four gradient descent towards the loading bay doors. The cargo had to be taken off the back of the trailer using a pallet truck and all efforts at levelling the deck using the adjustable suspension were in vain. On a rainy day with a wet trailer floor, it was a white knuckle ride, to say the least. The moment you placed the pallet truck beneath the pallet and lifted it more than one centimetre off the floor, the whole pallet would drag you and the pallet truck sliding towards the open doors. On more than one occasion I must have resembled a startled three year old taking the family Doberman for walkies!

Using a tail-lift for the first time can be a steep learning curve and there is a certain knack to it. Safety is paramount particularly when offloading in an area frequented by pedestrians and car drivers and these days, manufacturers fit their tail-lifts with safety bars and little ramps at the end of the tail lift which the driver engages whilst in use in the hope that he will not fall off the end and experience the terror of having his cargo follow him.

Nevertheless, there is no cure for stupid and I have experienced incidents where people have actually walked beneath my tail-lift as I was lowering it. On one occasion I was making a delivery to the front of a store in a high street. I was parked kerbside in the loading area and as I pushed my fully loaded pallet truck along the deck of the lorry towards my open trailer doors and raised tail-lift, some fool actually parked their car beneath the end of my raised tail-lift, got out of their vehicle and walked away, leaving me and my loaded pallet truck quite literally stranded in mid-air.

More than once I have had to prevent pedestrians from walking over my lowered tail-lift and vehicles parking on top of it as I was actually making my delivery.

Unsurprisingly, around 2,000 people are injured every year as a result of falling from a vehicle whilst loading or unloading and around 5,000 people are killed or injured every year as a result of objects falling from vehicles.

I have heard tell of many incidents whereby a driver was seriously injured falling from a tail lift or having part of their cargo collapse on top of them whilst unloading. Even loading bays have their drawbacks and the driver forums are littered with tales of woe, everything from drivers pulling away from a loading bay with the fork lift driver still in the back of the trailer to a story of one young lad who decided he needed a better view of the bay he was reversing onto and decided to open his drivers' side door. With his seatbelt disengaged, he leaned out, over-balanced and fell head first onto the tarmac. He was apparently out cold for several hours.

Other than slow manoeuvring a vehicle, unloading or loading and then securing cargo are situations where newbie drivers are most likely to make mistakes and even when things are going well the unexpected can still take you by surprise.

When I first started and was very uncertain about safe loading or strapping I often found myself using a veritable spider's web of straps, trying to ensure that everything was correctly secured. This once proved to be my undoing whilst delivering frozen goods in a 3.5-tonne truck. I had just finished making my delivery in a downpour and was soaked through to the skin. I then entered the rear of the vehicle to secure the cargo before leaving and was in there for so long that my hair and eyebrows froze. Even my nostril hair turned crispy. Before that day, I didn't even know such a thing was possible and it took the best part of the afternoon to get warm again. The nostril hair, however, never fully recovered and to this day, I am far from hirsute in that department.

THE YAWNING MOUTH OF BOREDOM

As a child, I used to keep a diary and from the age of nine my diary entries were filled with entertaining gems such as "Went to Paula's house and taught her dogs to puissance" and "Cycled to the pond to collect tadpoles" and in one astonishing admission "Must ask Dad what a blow job is".

Yes, it will come as no surprise that I was considered a tomboy and a fairly precocious one at that but oddly, the most common theme shot through the colours of my childhood scribblings was more often than not, one which indicated a stultifying level of boredom.

No doubt if my energies had been better channelled, I could have accomplished far greater things with my time but it was not to be. I have yet to paint a masterpiece or finish an epic novel (though I am working on that one) and today, I bitterly regret afternoons lost to pointless endeavours and hours wasted completing tasks which should have been accomplished in full by others, or not bothered with at all.

Boredom is very much a part of trucking life and filling time becomes something of a mission for all of us. In days gone by, drivers depended heavily upon paperback books, newspapers and whilst driving, a dashboard covered in mix tapes or CDs. With the advent of Kindle, Audible and YouTube, entire libraries of both books and music have become accessible to us at the touch of a phone screen and with many new trucks fitted with Bluetooth, these can be played through the sound systems of our vehicles. Never before has the trucker been provided with so many varied ways in which he can spend (or waste) his time.

My personal Audible library currently contains over two hundred titles and it is not unknown for me to plough through an entire novel in less than a week. Then of course there are the music and video streaming services, the podcasts, the 'listen again' services provided by many radio stations not to mention the social media platforms.

Gone are the days of digging through my work bag whilst trying to drive in a straight line along the M5 at night, fingers searching hungrily for my favourite mixtape with which to accompany me on my lonely travels. Instead, I simply shout at the dashboard of my truck to activate YouTube music via Bluetooth in order to access my favourite tunes to sing along to as I traverse the dark and winding roads of Great Britain.

The ways in which a driver can entertain himself during the hours of his daily shift are many and varied. I know of at least two drivers in my depot who bring guitars to work with them and practice their skills up and down the fretboard during their lunch breaks. Last year, I purchased a portable folding Bluetooth keyboard which connects to my phone and upon which I have tapped out several pages of this book in my idle moments.

Some drivers practice learning a new language, enjoy documentary podcasts or play silly games with themselves (such as counting wind turbines or yellow cars).

A good friend of mine who each week, works from late in the evening until the sun comes up, by way of making her shift more interesting, often avoids the motorways, taking instead the roads less travelled on her journey through the dark and lonely night.

To a trucker, boredom is more than an unpleasant inconvenience, it is a killer. It is a very short ride along a very slippery slope from boredom, to sleepiness, to "Oh my God, I nearly hit that car!"

Drivers spend an awful lot of time waiting at depots either for an available loading bay or to be loaded or unloaded. For those who find that sleep comes easy to them, in a depot filled with bright yard lights, vehicles starting up, reverse alarms sounding and engines revving, they will often be found taking forty winks on the bunk.

Unfortunately, as a light sleeper, I am not one of these drivers. Even with earplugs and an eye mask, a quick snooze is almost out of the realms of possibility for me, no matter how tired I may be or how long the wait.

One evening spent waiting for an available bay in the loading area of a commercial bakery was particularly memorable. It was around seven in the evening and already dark. The yard was dimly lit and I watched with interest as one of the factory floor staff pushed a wheelie bin full of overbaked bread across the space in front of me towards the compactor. Suddenly he froze in his tracks and I felt the hair rise on the back of my neck as a large brown rat the size of a small dog ran across the yard in front of my truck. Any thoughts I may have harboured of taking a nap during my wait were quickly dispelled in that moment.

I have also known of more than one driver who, whilst working a night shift and being faced with a very long wait at a depot, decided to get some well-deserved rest and slept so heavily that he did not awake until the sun was high in the sky the next morning. The importance of setting an alarm cannot be too heavily overstated here.

Many sites do not even permit the driver to remain in the vehicle whilst loading or unloading takes place and instead provide a 'driver rest area' where all breaks must be taken. Facilities supplied for use by the driver in these spaces can vary widely from those with kitchen areas or even fully serviced to canteens to a cold, noisy room with uncomfortable, hard plastic chairs and a vending machine (if you are lucky).

More often than not though, the driver can remain in their vehicle though they will sometimes be required to surrender their keys to the transport office or warehouse. Fortunately, this does not usually prevent the driver from charging his phone nor does it interfere with the workings of the cab heater.

Nevertheless, no one likes to be kept waiting and truckers are no exception.

Delays due to vehicle or trailer breakdowns and defects are also a common occurrence and a source of great annoyance to truckers. A wait in excess of two hours for attendance or repair is not unusual, adding to an already long and arduous day. The longest wait I have experienced while waiting for a breakdown truck was three hours but the longest time I have ever spent waiting for my load was one of six hours though I have heard of drivers who have waited far longer.

There is of course another downside to all of this. With so much entertainment at our fingertips, and many of us being paid by the hour, I fear that we have become too sanguine about being made to wait for the best part of half a day for our cargo. This in turn has allowed companies to further cut costs by employing fewer warehouse staff, surely an example of false economy since all of that time spent waiting has to be paid for by some-one, somewhere, further down the line towards the consumer or further up the chain of command towards the haulier himself.

With all of this technology, I feel that some part of truck driver 'culture' has been lost. In days gone by, drivers kept waiting for any length of time would have gathered in the yard for a chat to pass the time, chewing the fat, shooting the breeze and passing on stories, news, words of wisdom or advice to other drivers. Pull into any transport yard today and you will find drivers sitting in their cabs, talking on their phones, using social media or watching movies. They will pass hours in this manner, speaking to no one and aware of nothing that is going on around them.

The advance of technology, it seems, carries a price tag and that price is paid by the loss of good manners, desire for company and our duty towards the well-being of our own kind.

CHECK IT OUT

Driving a truck is not quite as straightforward as many would believe. When most people get into their car to begin their daily commute, they simply turn the key, drive out of their parking spot and head off to work with little consideration for the condition of their vehicle. Most are unlikely even to check the inflation of their tyres, the operation of their lights or their fluid levels but all of these, and more, must be checked by the trucker before he drives anywhere.

Some haulage companies will have many site policies regarding the checking of vehicles. These can include but are not limited to:

The amount of time which must be taken for vehicle checks
The order in which these should be done
The items which must be examined
The importance of not being distracted whilst checks are taking place

There is an almost inexhaustive list of tasks which a driver must complete at the start of his shift. This usually begins with signing in (with his signature or a swipe card) before downloading his digital tachograph card and receiving his keys and paperwork.

Only then does the fun begin, starting with a 'truck hunt'. If you work for a particularly large company with an expansive yard, and a fleet of vehicles painted only in one colour, this can take a good five or ten minutes and involves walking around the place, franticly pressing on a key fob and hoping that something will flash its lights at you. If you are fortunate, you may have a key fob with an alarm button which once pressed, will sound the horn of your truck allowing you to home in on its location.

Once you have your vehicle, have placed your bag inside the cab and inserted your digital tachograph card into the reader (not forgetting, of course, to make your manual tachograph record entries) it is time to don your gloves and perform your 'walk-around checks.

These would usually begin with tyres, checking for good inflation, tread wear, wheel nut movement and tyre or wheel damage before moving onto the lights. A tractor unit has far more of these than any car and all of them must be operational and undamaged. Most truckers are trained in the changing of bulbs but with the advent of LED lights, the necessity for this is becoming less frequent. Trucks are also fitted with extremely complex diagnostics systems which can either be terribly helpful or incredibly annoying. They will inform you when you have a bulb blown but they will just as easily sound a constant and highly irritating alarm when (for example) your seat belt is working fine but the seat belt sensor is having a bad day.

The driver would also check the condition of the fuel and ad-blue caps, the state of his air and electrical leads, the security of the spray suppression (mud flaps) and make a visual check of anything else which may be bolted to the outside of his tractor unit.

He would then move on to checking the fluid levels (oil, coolant and windscreen fluid) which may necessitate either a physical check beneath the bonnet of the truck or a diagnostic check from within the cab. This complete, he or she would then arrange the inside of the cab to suit. The seat position should be set, the mirrors (of which there are usually at least six) should be cleaned and correctly positioned and all loose items safely stowed.

He should, in addition, make certain that he has been supplied with a trailer number plate and any other additional equipment that he would need for his particular line of work.

Finally, a dashboard gauge and diagnostic check is required since leaving your yard in a brand new vehicle, no company fuel card and an almost empty fuel tank does not generally make you popular. Particularly when you drive 60 miles up the M5 and the fuel light comes on. (Yes, I have actually done this).

So once you and your tractor unit are ready and raring to go, it's time to find your trailer! This usually necessitates a slow drive around the yard, muttering trailer numbers to yourself and trying not to be so distracted that you either hit an unwary pedestrian or drive into something.

Once found, you would position your tractor unit so that its rear is properly square and lined up with the front of the trailer. Most importantly, the driver would now apply his handbrake and get out of the tractor unit to check that the trailer brake has been applied (this should have been undertaken by the previous driver who parked that particular trailer but this is not a given). I can recall one occasion where I witnessed a driver rather carelessly and forcefully reversing the rear of his tractor unit beneath the front of his trailer, only to find that the trailer brake had not been applied, and the whole ensemble jumped rearwards by about six inches and smashed into the wall of the warehouse.

In addition to this, if the trailer was parked on a loading bay, the driver would check first to make sure that the trailer was not being loaded or unloaded. Many companies have very strict policies which prevent drivers from coupling or uncoupling their tractor units whilst loading or unloading is taking place. There are good reasons for this. Seven percent of all forklift and powered pallet truck accidents occur due to trailers being pulled away from a bay whilst the trailer is still being loaded. This figure was once much higher but recent HSE innovations involving traffic light systems on loading bays, truck airline coupling locks and the application of trailer wheel chocks have done much to reduce these incidents.

Before reversing his tractor unit beneath his trailer, the driver would do a quick visual check of its condition, looking for obvious defects. He may also open the rear doors of the trailer or (if permitted) enter the warehouse to check the safety of his load. He or she would check the security and tautness of load retaining bars or straps and those straps which secure the curtains (if pulling a curtain-sided trailer).

Once safely reversed beneath the trailer, the driver would apply the safety clip to the king-pin mechanism. This ensures that the trailer and tractor unit are correctly coupled, though a quick visual check with a good torch shone between the jaws of the fifth wheel plate in addition, does not go amiss.

Next comes my least favourite part as this is where the driver is most likely to get him or herself covered in that most unpleasant of substances, fifth-wheel grease. Here, the driver has to climb up a set of steps at the rear of the cab onto a metal platform known as the catwalk and insert his air leads and electric leads into the couplings on the front of his trailer. The space between the cab and the trailer can sometimes be rather cramped and the air-line couplings hard to insert since they are air pressurised.

A thorough greasing avoided, the driver dismounts from the catwalk backwards. This is an important point as dismounting forward from the catwalk, catching your foot on the last rung of the steps and face-planting in a most undignified manner in the middle of a busy yard, is not a good look.

The next step of the process involves winding up the legs of your trailer using a good old fashioned winding handle, a low tech piece of equipment which rarely fails but can still cause an extraordinary amount of trouble. They can break, bend, get stuck in difficult positions and the clips which hold them in place regularly fall off, leaving the driver with no choice but to secure them to the undercarriage of the trailer using shrink wrap, cable ties or anything else he may have to hand.

The last part of the coupling process ends with the driver disengaging the trailer brake. This is usually a red button, close to the leg winding handle but can sometimes be found at the front of the trailer. If the driver has remembered to apply his handbrake inside the cab, all will be well. If not, he will be left chasing his runaway truck down the yard.

Next, the driver must raise the suspension of the trailer and thoroughly check around the wheels and tyres, looking out for wheel nut movement, low tyre tread depth, cuts and gouges,

bulges, flat spots, poor inflation and really anything which shouldn't be there. Since the tyres and
wheels are the only part of any vehicle which is in
contact with the road, they are probably the most
important component.

A tyre blowout is a terrifying experience
and with truck tyres being pressurised to 125psi,
when they burst, the sound is like that of a gun fir-
ing at close range.

Finally, the driver must return his trailer
and tractor unit suspension to normal travelling
height and lower his lift-axels (if travelling fully
loaded). These are axels on the tractor unit or
trailer which can be raised to travel in the up position when the trailer is empty to cut down on tyre
wear.

They can only be adjusted when the ignition is switched on and the air systems within
the tractor unit and trailer are fully pressurised.
These air systems also control the operation of the
suspension, clutch, brakes, gears, ABS systems and
many more besides (including the suspension of
the driver's seat).

I was recently told a tale of one particular driver who had started his engine in order to
pressurise the air systems within his tractor unit
and trailer and was performing some additional
checks beside his lift axel when the engine cut
out. Many newer vehicles are set to cut out after
three minutes in order to prevent prolonged idling
and to help reduce emissions. Unfortunately for

this particular driver, the lift axel which had been in the raised position, did not have enough air pressure to remain raised and automatically began lowering, trapping the foot of the driver beneath it. Fortunately, he was wearing a pair of sturdy steel toe capped boots and after several hours of waving frantically at the security cameras in an empty yard, he was mercifully rescued by another driver. No doubt he was late home that evening with quite the story to tell.

THE GREASY SPOON

Layovers and stopping points have existed in this country in one form or another since the end of the Iron age and possibly before.

In the UK, facilities for truckers can be divided into two categories, those which provide formal, overnight parking and those which do not.

Traditionally, transport cafes were situated in lay-by's or close to the roadside so that parking could sometimes be extremely limited to perhaps no more than half a dozen spaces for trucks. Some older and more established cafes have since been able to expand over the years and now provide a small formal parking area and although they are usually located mostly along the old coaching routes and A-roads of Great Britain, their customers are no longer only restricted truck drivers. Some have branched out further and are now considered to be Truck Stops rather than transport cafes alone, providing facilities which may include showers, a small shop, fuel and even laundry facilities. Others have taken the up-market 'gastro' route to appeal to a wider variety of clientele.

The Romans were the first to fully understand the need for respite from the travails of the road, providing accommodation, beer and a hearty meal for all Romans or Romano-Britons who were willing or able to pay for such things. Their horses (should they have arrived with horses rather than on foot) would also be fed, rested and groomed, their tack cleaned and their harnesses checked for damage and wear.

During the times of Post-Romano Britain, every monastery and convent along every well-worn route would have provided safe harbour within its walls for those seeking rest and refreshment but the first coaching inns were not to be established until the late middle ages. Astonishingly, a very small number of those ancient buildings are still in existence today as restaurants or hotels.

The very first coffee house was established in Oxford in 1652 and it is believed that the first transport cafés specifically aimed towards providing facilities for truck drivers became established in the 1930s. A very small number of these have continued to provide food and limited parking for truckers for the best part of ninety years, through the bombing raids of the 1940s and the advent of the very first motorway service station at Watford Gap on the M1 in 1959.

A survey in 1960 found that there were over one thousand independent transport cafes in the UK but this golden era was about to come to an abrupt end with the provision of dedicated lorry parks and truckers cafés within the boundaries of many motorway service areas during the 1960s and '70s which preceded the inevitable decline in passing A-road haulage traffic. Many transport cafes closed, others sold their long-established family business to large organisations such as Happy Eater and Little Chef in the 1980s. Both companies prohibited trucks from parking on their premises, ringing the death knell of the traditional Transport Café and driving most truckers onto the tarmac of the motorway service station lorry park.

Western Europe takes a quite different view towards truck drivers and works hard to make them feel much more welcome. Pull into any motorway service station in France and you are unlikely to be charged for spending the night there. France also provides smaller parking areas along its autoroutes and A-road equivalents, with one every 15 miles or so. These are called 'Aires', are always free and usually come with toilets and other basic facilities.

Although much of Europe charges for the use of its Autoroutes, the cost of using the motorway facilities is generally kept low. Showers will usually be cleaner, more numerous and the food will be of a higher quality.

There have also been efforts in recent times to revive the fortunes of British transport cafés and truckstops. These efforts have been greatly assisted by the total indifference with which truckers are now regarded by many of the larger motorway service station organisations, evident by their high parking tariffs, the high cost or poor nutritive quality of food provided, the distant proximity of toilets, the insufficient number of clean showering facilities and the lack of secure premises.

But in order to keep these small independent companies from disappearing altogether, they absolutely **must be used!**

It is up to us as drivers to support these organisations and favour the dedicated attention and hard work of the truckstop and transport café over the convenient but impersonal charms of the motorway service station.

There exists now probably fewer than 250 traditional truckstops and transport cafes in the UK, a sad cry from the heydays of the 1960s but perhaps the advent of technology could be the saviour of these independent establishments.

Apps such as Intruck or Snap and websites such as www.transportcafe.co.uk provide the driver with the all-important information required to make an informed choice regarding his (or her) stopover arrangements. They list the number of parking spaces available, whether or not the site provides showers or fueling facilities, whether or not there is CCTV and the full contact details for the site (including the all-important postcode). A quick google search may also show additional information including reviews, images and ease of access data for larger vehicles.

The image of the 'greasy spoon' café may not have been the best in times gone by but there is today a new, younger breed of trucker with expectations far beyond that of a dirty shower and a full English breakfast. The truckstops and cafes which have survived competition from the motorway service stations have done so by offering more than that which is offered by the likes of Moto and Welcome Break and the new driver should not be fooled by an uncomplicated façade or smaller parking area than that which the big boys provide.

Some of my most memorable stopovers have been taken at these smaller truckstops and transport cafes. Long before I learned to drive, my family made an annual pilgrimage to visit my grandmother in north Wales. Since my father disliked the dull uniformity of the M6 in the 1970s, our route would take us north along the M5 and onto the M4, crossing the old Severn Bridge and into Chepstow. We would then follow the green and leafy roads through the Wye Valley and north towards Hereford, Shrewsbury and Llangollen before stopping at a transport café on the top of the Horseshoe Pass. There, my parents would drink tea and my sister and I would feed the last of our sandwiches to the tame sheep which hung around the car park waiting for bored little girls with a soft spot for anything woolly, before dropping down off the hills and onwards to Rhyl, our final destination.

Incredibly, the café, called the Ponderosa, is still there though I am unsure about parking provision for trucks, however, according to Google maps, the lay-by opposite certainly has potential.

These traditional establishments have for many years (and in some cases, many decades) kept their clients happy, well-fed and ready to face the day. They understand the needs of the driver and they have adapted to those needs over the years. As tastes and requirements have changed, the truckstops and transport cafes have kept pace and today it is not unusual to walk into a truckstop and discover laundry services, rooms to rent for the night and shops selling everything a trucker could ever need, alongside the usual café, showers, and toilets, all of these offered at a far lower price than that of the average motorway service station.

Perhaps the reluctance of some drivers to use these sites in the past could be attributed to a lack of consistency and lack of information. Some sites may offer only parking, food, toilets and little else. Others provided the full gamut of facilities and it is up to us as tech-savvy drivers to make use of the data that is available to us at the swipe of a phone screen. Where possible, we should choose to favour the little guy, to keep these businesses thriving in order to retain the handful of organisations dedicated to the wellbeing of drivers rather than pour our hard-earned cash into swelling the coffers of the multinationals.

Unless we lend our support to smaller entities, we may find ourselves in the same position as our continental brethren who must bring all of their food with them through Europe, cooking and preparing their meals using their little outdoor stoves and parking in lay-by's and on industrial estates. The reason for this seemingly odd behaviour is not born of dislike for British food tastes (though that may also play a part) but one born of the need to economise. The disparity in wages between that of the British trucker and the Eastern European driver is so great that our continental friends are simply priced out of the market. Their wages, considered acceptable in their country of origin, are thoroughly inadequate to cover the cost of trucking in the UK. A driver in the Czech Republic would typically earn the equivalent of £600 per month, an average motorway service station would relieve a driver of around £30 per night and when you add to this the cost of food in many of these places, you can understand why most choose to bring their own food and seek free stop-overs in the sorts of places that the British trucker would consider the 'port of last resort'.

However, as British drivers, we may be missing a trick here. As we retreat alone into our cosy cabs with our laptops, talking to no one and ignoring our neighbours, our continental friends will be sitting together at the rear of their trucks, sharing their home-cooked food, swapping stories, laughing and networking like the British truckers of old before the days of motorways, mobile phones and Netflix.

I would not suggest that we should return to that way of life, after all, the march of time carries us all before it but perhaps we should not take for granted that which may not be around forever should we neglect to make use of it.

THE WRONG
SIDE OF THE LAW

The haulage industry is one of the most heavily regulated industries in the UK. Anyone involved in the transportation of goods by road can face pretty serious consequences should anything go horribly wrong. It isn't just the driver who faces penalties for making mistakes but also his employer.

Drivers are of course, responsible for ensuring that they follow the highway code as well as their own common sense. They must conform to Drivers Hours Regulations as the Road Transport Directive regarding working hours regulations, they must ensure that their vehicle is roadworthy and safe to drive and that the load is secure but that is not all there is to doing this job. It is easy to accidentally fall foul of the law and inexperienced drivers do this all the time.

As I have already mentioned, Driving hour, working hour and tachograph regulations are extremely complex. They can be simplified into a few simple maxims which most drivers can remember but certain situations can add further levels of confusion and uncertainty to those unfamiliar with the rules. I will not delve further into this here since I am aware that some of you may not be truck drivers, suffice to say that it is estimated that in any 28-day period, 20% of all vehicles being driven on UK and EU roads will have, on record, at least one minor infringement. Most would be situations where the driver has failed to stop at the correct time for a mandatory break following four and a half hours of driving or six hours of working. He may not have taken enough breaks during the day or between shifts. He may have worked or driven for longer than he should have and all drivers make these mistakes. It is often nothing more than an accidental miscalculation though this is becoming less likely as technology advances and many trucks now display a dashboard warning should the driver be about to exceed his or her driving or working limits.

A more serious category of infringements would include, failure to insert a tachograph card or failure to provide tachograph records to an enforcement officer should these be requested.

The first category of infringements could carry a fine of up to £2,500, the latter and more serious category could cost a driver double that figure though most drivers do not deliberately, knowingly or persistently commit any of these offences and therefore are unlikely to face fines or prosecution though they could face a verbal warning should a mild offence come to light following roadside checks by the Driver and Vehicle Standards Agency (DVSA).

It also has to be said that some employers do not make it easy for drivers to remain within the law. In times gone by, most transport planners were usually ex-drivers themselves who understood the amount of time it would take for a truck to get from point A to point B. They knew that the driver may have to wait to be loaded or unloaded or that at certain times of day he would encounter heavy traffic and a good planner would make allowances for these delays when calculating the driver's route. Not only must a planner be aware of how the day is likely to pan out for each trucker, he must also understand drivers' hour's regulations back to front and inside out.

Any good transport office still employs only ex-drivers as planners but increasingly, those who would not know one end of a truck from another are being awarded these positions and it shows. Walk into any haulage company which is well run, with little stress and you will usually find that ex-truckers are in charge but if you walk into any situation where this is not the case, you will find exasperated drivers, aggravated office staff and clients who are slowly losing the will to live.

All road haulage companies themselves must also conform to an overabundance of rules, regulations and restrictions. These would include:

Ensuring that vehicles are serviced and MOT'd correctly and on time.

Any and all vehicle defects are reported and fixed promptly or immediately, depending upon severity.

All staff are correctly trained in the use of their equipment and the rules of the site.

That the site is safe, clean and properly maintained.

And that all employees and visitors conform to all regulations regarding the correct operation of the site.

Most larger haulage firms will employ more than one Operators Licence (O-Licence) holder (the individual responsible for maintaining the fleet) and at least one Compliance Officer whose unenviable job it is to make sure that everyone plays by the rules.

Any well-run haulage operation is run 'bottom heavy' with plenty of drivers, warehouse staff, forklift and powered pallet truck drivers, trainers and assessors, admin staff, team leaders and booking-in staff. This is where the majority of the work lies since this is a 'body on the shop floor' orientated industry. Middle and upper management numbers should be kept light since if the staff lower down the food chain are numerous and well trained, staff turnover will be minimal, the work will get done properly and on time and everyone goes home happy, including the upper management who can simply do their job with little inter-ruption. The increasing trend towards paying high salaried managers or consultants and running the shop floor at minimal staff capacity is a dangerous one. This results in overstressed and overworked employees, a very high staff turnover, work which is never completed safely or on time, rules being bent, regulations being broken and the eventual liquidation of the site.

Haulage companies sometimes need to be reminded that if they take good care of their staff, the staff will go the extra mile for the customer and for their employer.

No driver will remain for long with a company that forces him to constantly work to his maximum hours, with start or finish times that do not suit him, driving dirty vehicles with defect warnings lighting up the dashboard like Blackpool illuminations or to unrealistic deadlines which just leave him feeling demoralised.

I have often been expected to do all of these things and more and it has to be said that sometimes drivers do themselves no favours by tolerating such nonsense. It just makes it harder for the rest of us to maintain high standards across the board.

What one driver will tolerate sets a precedent for all others in the eyes of their employer.

There are several situations within driver hours and route planning regulations that drivers can fall foul of if they are unaware of their rights.

The driver is responsible for his own fitness to drive but it is not unknown for planners to coerce drivers into reducing their standard daily rest from eleven to nine hours (this is the rest that drivers must take in-between shifts).

This coercion is not permitted under law, the driver must agree willingly to reduce his rest and should never be forced since he is responsible for any and all mistakes made the following day should he be too tired to perform his duties safely and to the best of his ability. I have been made aware of many situations too where drivers were regularly planned for a fifteen-hour day which can create a forced reduced daily rest should the driver's start time the next day be the same as the day before. This is illegal, poor practice and reckless in the extreme but it is up to drivers themselves to say no to this sort of bullying. These situations sometimes arise as a result of ignorance on the part of both the planner and the driver but equally, planners may sometimes be all too aware of what they are doing.

The sort of work I perform today rarely requires me to reduce my rest or to work to my maximum driving or shift hours, I am also well aware that the DVSA (formally known as VOSA) are always on the lookout for drivers who are pushing themselves to their limits and of the companies which force them into doing so.

The other ways in which a driver can fall foul of the law come in the form of vehicle defects or unsafe loading and strapping. Most of the time this is due to either poor training on the part of the employer or inexperience or carelessness on the part of the driver or loading staff, but once again, it is up to the driver to speak out and take action if something does not look or feel right.

If, like one driver who contacted me, you are given a trailer where two out of three hinges on a trailer door have come loose and are hanging in mid-air, you should not be expected by your transport manager to cover the defect with duct tape and get on your way. In this situation, a trucker must stand his ground and refuse to take the trailer. If his manager continues to insist, he should probably seek a new employer forthwith.

Many years ago, I took employment with a small firm, delivering and collecting skips in the local area. On my first day with the company whilst descending a steep hill, I braked to slow down on the approach to a pedestrian crossing. Nothing happened and when I say nothing, I mean absolutely nothing. Terrified, I rose in my seat and practically stamped upon the pedal. The vehicle slowed slightly but not enough to actually stop. Mercifully, nobody was standing upon the crossing as my truck flew over it.

It finally came to halt at the end of the road, whereupon I turned it around and gingerly drove it back up the hill and into the yard.

My new transport manager was mystified as to why I had returned so soon and even after

I explained the situation, he still appeared rather surprised when I refused to drive the truck. I walked out of the job then and there, having been employed by that company for no more than one hour. I looked back as I got to the car park to find the manager handing the keys of the truck to another driver who had just arrived to start his shift. I watched as the driver left, loaded up with an empty skip for delivery and made a very discreet and anonymous phone call to VOSA.

Several months later I was informed that the company had gone into liquidation following an investigation that found serious defects on every vehicle in the fleet and a catalogue of site Health and Safety violations.

Rules, regulations and high standards exist for a reason. Imagine the consequences should someone have been using the crossing that day. I would have lost my licence and my liberty, my employer would have suffered a similar fate and the chances are that some poor pedestrian would have lost their life. Trucks are potential murder machines and they must be maintained with care and treated with the greatest of respect at all times.

RITES OF PASSAGE

Male truckers have something of a reputation when it comes to the ladies. They are often perceived as being sexist, middle-aged philanderers with a roving eye and a lover in every town. The truth, however, is that the horizontal habits of many of us could not be more conventional.

Sure, if a truck driver, regardless of their gender, insists that they have never used their cab for less orthodox purposes, they are probably lying. If they are being truthful they will almost certainly wish they were not, though as with many of life's little fantasies, the reality rarely meets with expectation.

Attempting anything more adventurous than sleep on a bed measuring no more than around 3ft in width requires a level of planning and improvisation worthy of a military campaign, more so if your company does not see fit to provide you with the luxury of a high cab in which you can stand upright.

Many drivers who spend any time sleeping

in their truck are usually too exhausted at the end of a hard day to consider anything more adventurous than a phone call to their spouse and a cup of hot cocoa whilst watching a movie but for those spending a night in the truck closer to home, it was not unknown in the past, for a driver to call their partner over to the truckstop for an evening of passion on the bunk.

The days of parking up for the night and spending the evening getting drunk at a local establishment followed by a night of illicit (and possibly paid-for) sex in the lorry, are long gone, if they ever existed in the first place. With the increase in incidents of hijacking, most drivers would be under strict instructions, on pain of instant dismissal, not to invite any individual other than a fellow employee of the same company, into their vehicle. As for a night on the lash? It goes without saying that an employer would take a very dim view of any driver found to be over the legal alcohol limit in charge of a truck, regardless of whether or not they were actually driving it.

All these restrictions, rules and regulations do not, however, prevent any naughty nocturnal happenings from taking place. Spend any time working shifts which require you to take daily rests in your vehicle and you will encounter lorry park sex-workers (commonly known by the highly derogatory title of 'Lot Lizards' in the USA).

These unfortunate individuals make a living plying their trade in the large truckstops and motorway service areas of the UK late at night and in all weathers. Are they exploited? Are they trafficked? Quite possibly. After all, it is not the kind of job that anyone would volunteer for and they probably make slim pickings amongst the British drivers who may only be away for one or two nights in every week, though amongst our continental brethren, who spend far longer away from home, perhaps the trade is more lucrative, who knows?

This said, truckers can be a strange breed and a partner in crime is not always required in order to satisfy one's more carnal desires.

When I asked my friends and the online community for their trucking tales, I was somewhat surprised concerning the sheer volume of stories, along the line of horizontal happenings, which flooded my inbox.

One of these was of a trucker who stopped for his regulation break, reversed into a space in a very small lorry park, changed his tachograph mode to 'rest' and happened to glance across into the cab next to him to find the driver performing an act of self-relief in broad daylight with little regard for his new neighbour. Disgusted by the view, the driver left the lorry park post-haste, preferring to incur a tachograph infringement rather than be subjected to that particular solo performance.

I was given several stories which followed a similar theme. On one occasion the driver got out of his truck and in a fit of rage, dragged the offending driver from his cab and punched him square in the middle of his meat and two veg, so it just goes to prove that truckers can be a fairly conservative bunch who object strongly to louche behaviour when it is on show for all to see.

This doesn't mean that all truckers are as dull as ditchwater. One driver told me that he was once handed the keys to his vehicle by a lady driver who had occupied that particular lorry for several days. Later that afternoon and upon further examination of the truck, to his alarm, he discovered her secret stash of vibrating gadgets, confiding that at least one of these items looked as though it should have been 'plugged into the mains'.

My inbox was flooded with tales of drivers being 'flashed' either whilst driving or whilst sitting in a lay-by. Both men and women were the recipients of this sort of attention. Occasionally it was welcomed, sometimes it most certainly was not.

I also received a few stories of 'things once seen, which cannot be unseen'. The view from a truck is a pretty expansive one and that which escapes the attention of a car driver, does not escape the all-seeing eye of the average trucker.

Open the door to the cab of a modern truck and the floor inside will be level with your shoulders or above. With some types of high-cab truck, I have to jump off the ground to reach the grab handles, which are positioned to the left and right of the door and provide the driver with stability as he mounts the steps into the cab. Add the height of a seat and the height of the seated driver to that equation and you will understand how broad our view is.

I have witnessed at least one car driver receiving pleasure from his passenger as he negotiated the highways of England and one trucker told me of a similar incident that involved a truck driver and his companion from whom he was accepting a particularly enjoyable oral conversation. Another story which caught my attention was of a trucker who happened to find himself following a vehicle belonging to a well-known supermarket chain along the M6. It was late in the evening and the vehicle was weaving a little and frequently veering towards the hard shoulder. Assuming that driver fatigue was to blame for such erratic behaviour, the trucker made sure to allow plenty of room as he overtook on a steep hill but as he glanced across into the cab of the other driver, he was alarmed to notice that the weaving and drifting was caused by the fact that he was watching porn on his tablet and acting out his fantasies as he drove!

I was told of one unfortunate driver, who having parked up for the night, came to the gradual realisation that he had stopped his vehicle in a lay-by commonly used for the activity known as 'dogging' and for those of you with a nervous disposition and who are unaware of what that word means, may I strongly urge you not to 'Google' it.

It appears that laybys are not only occupied by tired drivers hoping for a little rest and recuperation. There are many stories of drivers of both sexes being harassed by men and occasionally women who are hoping for a little roadside action. I was even told one story of a chap who was approached by another gentleman wearing nothing but the sort of black, revealing underwear not usually associated with the male sex.

It does seem that when one is cosseted within a metal and glass box on wheels, one experiences a level of security out of all proportion to the reality of one's situation. Instances of those who witness others committing acts of indecent exposure (or worse) whilst either behind the wheel of a vehicle or whilst reclining in the passenger seat, are shockingly commonplace.

I do not think I need to remind anyone of the potential risks to life and limb (or other appendages) involved by undertaking such activity whilst driving, let alone the humiliation of coming before the Traffic Commissioner (no pun intended) should one be caught in the act.

STRANGER
THINGS

In the course of our careers, most truckers will clock up an average of around 100,00 miles every year. Over the course of a lifetime that can be as much as four and a half million miles. To the moon and back over nine times!

Many of us have some strange tales to tell of odd things that we have seen or experienced whilst driving, for my part, I'm sorry to say that I have barely a handful of weird and wonderful stories to relay regarding odd or inexplicable things which I have seen on the road. Probably the only one which made me almost laugh myself out of the cab was an incident on the M5 when I was passed by a small car modified to resemble a Duracell battery with the sunroof rolled back. This was being driven and co-piloted by two young men wearing pink, fluffy Duracell bunny suits (including ears) whilst headbanging to some very loud rock music.

In my supermarket delivery days, I often found myself collecting from a large regional distribution centre in Willand, north Devon. On this particular day, the site was very busy and I was asked to wait to be unloaded. I had been parked on the bay for around thirty minutes when I noticed that several members of the sparrow population kept approaching the front of the parked vehicles and flying between the gaps in the grill. I watched with amazement as each one of them left with a tasty insect morsel between their beaks. These clever creatures had figured out that if they waited patiently until each vehicle had cooled down, they could fly in and grab a free (if slightly squashed and cooked) meal from the front of the radiator.

On another occasion, whilst travelling between Cirencester and Swindon in a large rigid vehicle, I happened to look over the hedge to my left and briefly catch sight of a large black animal resembling a jaguar bounding through a wheat field. The beast of Bodmin on holiday perhaps? But it appears that I am not the only one to experience such things. When I couched the following question to the discussion board of several trucking forums "What weird or inexplicable things have you seen on the road?" some of the replies ranged from hilarious to alarming and all the way through to shocking and horrific.

There was one lovely story of how a mother duck and her babies brought junction 21 of the M6 to a standstill as they were escorted safely by the police across both carriageways and another tale of a huge herd of deer crossing the ten-lane section of the M25, all of them making it from one side to the other without incident.

One driver who was following behind a livestock trailer got the surprise of his life when a giraffe poked its head out of the rear hatch and glared at him.

A tale of a cow ambling down Baldock High Street and a story of a woman walking along Oxford Road in Clacton with a pig on a lead.

Another story was similar to one of mine and definitely caught my eye. A big cat sighting in 2001 on the B4215 between Gloucester and Newent at two o'clock in the morning on two consecutive nights. This was not only spotted by the driver but by their passenger as well.

This seems to be a regular occurrence for drivers, with sightings in both Derbyshire and Telford also.

A good friend of mine who used to be a truck driving instructor but has since retired and now runs a forum for lady truckers in the UK, told me of the time that whilst driving close to Epping Forest at 6 am on a cold clear morning, both she and her trainee witnessed a black panther leave the cover of dense forest and stroll nonchalantly across open grassland before re-entering the wood. Neither of them could quite believe what they had just seen and in broad daylight too.

I received another tale of two men seen on a bridge overlooking the M6 motorway, one dressed as Darth Vader and the other as Luke Skywalker, both engaged in a rather intense lightsaber battle (and no, that is not a euphemism).

Cosplay appears to be a running theme on the roads of Great Britain with one driver reported seeing a chap dressed as a kangaroo, being chased by the police along the hard shoulder of the M6 near Preston.

One guy saw a giant plastic stegosaurus being driven around the M25, strapped to the back of a flatbed trailer. Another time he spotted a flock of chickens strutting down the hard shoulder of the M4 and on a different day, two kids cycling along the M3. No doubt by this time, he was beginning to wonder if they were putting something in his coffee back at the depot.

Another driver found himself being highly entertained as he watched three people dressed as skeletons, dancing around a bus stop in a town centre.

Then of course there is the gentlemen who became rather famous for dressing as a Roman legionnaire and walking up and down the roads of Ferryhill and Thinford, County Durham.

Another driver told me of a time when he was waiting at a T-Junction and a guy crossed the road in front of him wearing a cowboy hat, boots, chaps and spurs pulling a small cart behind him, upon which was fixed a perch and upon that perch was sat an owl.

Several drivers mentioned a man seen wearing a kilt, standing in the middle of a field in Scotland playing the bagpipes, one guy saw a man playing the trumpet whilst sat in a queue of traffic and another was treated to a fellow trucker practising his violin whilst waiting for his vehicle to be loaded.

Quite a few individuals mentioned spotting both men and women in the early hours of the morning completing the 'walk of shame' wearing very little or nothing at all and another driver one day, had to give a wide berth to the commonwealth games cycling team out for a practice run early one morning near Leeds on the A1M in 2002.

On a darker note, there were tales of a knife fight in a customer's yard (both parties were arrested) and a story of one chap who passed a fireman, who following a fatality, was walking along the hard shoulder of the M6 carrying a severed human arm. Another incident involved a motorcyclist where the Motorcyclist's helmet was found still 'occupied' by the head of the rider.

One lady driver told me of how she had witnessed someone jumping from the Severn Bridge and on the same day was passed on the M4 by a man dressed as Santa Claus, riding a Honda Goldwing motorcycle covered in tinsel and fairy lights. A very strange day indeed!

Even the bodies of the deceased in their entirety have occasionally been found by members of the trucking community, as I say, the view from a truck is broad indeed and that which cannot be seen from a car, can clearly be seen from a truck and things which others believe they have hidden from view are occasionally discovered by those who truly wish they had never found them. From ladies underwear secreted in a truck driven only by male colleagues to human excrement unwittingly stepped on at night in a dark lay-by.

One lady driver told me of something she most certainly wished she had never seen one night when she parked her vehicle on the old Alconbury airfield. She had only been there a short while but was suddenly startled to see a young man striding into view wearing a long RAF coat and boots, looking like something straight out of WW2. The whole site is apparently rife with paranormal activity and the driver, convinced she had seen something wholly unnatural, turned her vehicle back around and drove straight out of there.

This is not the only 'supernatural' story I received. I was given this story by a retired truck driver and former police constable David Russell who is a regular contributor to Trucking Magazine.

Many years ago, there used to be an old roadhouse called The Punchbowl on the A66 at North Stainmore. It began to lose trade when that section of the A66 was upgraded to a dual carriageway, all but bypassing the establishment. One landlord attempted to halt the decline by creating an ad-hoc truck stop on the site offering free parking, showers, live music and great pub food. It soon became very popular and was regularly full to capacity every night.

Just to give you a little history here, the site was once a busy coaching inn with a chapel situated opposite. During times of religious unrest, the local priests were sometimes considered legitimate targets and as such, needed to have routes of escape from people wishing to do them harm. To this end, a tunnel was constructed beneath the road leading from a 'Priest Hole' in the chapel to the cellar of The Punch Bowl and hopefully on towards a route to salvation.

Forward in time many centuries later and it so happened that a group of drivers (including our erstwhile David Russell) became involved in a 'lock in' with the landlord and his good lady wife.

Stories were swapped and their host told them about the existence of the tunnel. The drivers were, of course, sceptical so the landlord offered to show them the actual tunnel. The assembled doubters descended into the cellar via a hatch and ladder. Unseen by them, the landlady descended by another route.

Grouped around the tunnel entrance, the landlord told a lurid tale of ghosts and spirits which were said to haunt the tunnel and invited the most gullible of their number to put his arm into the tunnel to feel the breeze.

As he waved his arm around in the darkness, it was seized by an unseen hand with an iron grip (the landlady having a laugh).

The scramble for the ladder after he screamed would be worthy of any Ealing Films comedy. Three less-than-athletic truck drivers trying to ascend the same ladder simultaneously.

It is alleged that the guy who was gripped got onto the ladder last and got off it first, passing the others on the way up.

Unfortunately, the popularity of the Punch Bowl and its colourful landlord, was not to last and following one incident where a trucker imbibed a little too heavily at the establishment before driving away and flipping his car transporter onto one side at Warcop, the truckstop became instead a regular haunt for the local constabulary hoping to raise their monthly breathalyser statistics and it finally called last orders on the trucking fraternity in the early 2000s.

I shall, however, end this chapter on a lighter note with a story from Wendy, a good friend of mine. This incident took place in 1982 when she was double manning with her then-partner, taking a load to Italy. ('Double manning' is where two drivers take it in turns to drive the vehicle).

The channel ferry they used that day had an image of an animal painted on the wall of each parking level (a giraffe for level one, a lion for level two etc.) so that you could easily remember which level you had parked on.

Their level had an elephant and curious, she asked her partner what this was all about. He told her it was because they were going to see an elephant on their trip. Of course, Wendy scoffed at his nonsense, hardly able to believe that he thought she would fall for that, but calling his bluff anyway, she kept the narrative going, making out that she believed him and continued to ask him all the way throughout their trip south, when she was going to see her elephant. They drove to Italy, delivered their cargo, collected a load for England and returned home via the scenic Mount Cenis in France. They parked in a lovely little truck stop on the top of the mountain and ordered food from the café.

Whilst they were waiting for their meal, a well-dressed gentleman entered the diner and called across the room "Who owns the Nichols truck out there?"

Her partner said, "That's us mate, what's the problem?"

His reply stunned them both.

"Can you move it forward a few yards so we can get our elephant out please?"

Of course, her partner immediately thought that Wendy had set him up and it took a while to convince him that this was absolutely not the case.

They trooped outside, followed by most of the, now very curious, clientele of the café. They moved their vehicle, the other man dropped the ramp of the livestock transporter and out stepped a gorgeous young elephant.

The story was that a film company was making a documentary about how Hannibal crossed the Alps with elephants and this little darling was one of the actors. Animal welfare regulations demanded that they made regular stops along the route so that their little star could eat, drink, rest and exercise.

For the remainder of the journey, Wendy's partner kept giving her the side-eye, convinced that she was possessed of some kind of magical power. "Honestly", she told me, "I couldn't have planned that incident better if I had tried!"

WHAT IT SAYS
ON THE TIN

Types of trucking work are many and varied and it can take a driver several years to find his or her niche. It really is a case of 'horses for courses' and what suits one driver will not always suit another. Even the shift patterns can vary greatly with some sites offering start times at every hour of the day and night, though it is best practice to keep each driver consistently set to a start time that works for them. Some companies operate shift start time windows and the driver will be given start times which vary only to within a few hours of each other from one day to the next. This works well for most since it keeps the body clock regular and reduces driver fatigue.

Many larger companies run a rolling week, though this is not popular with everyone. This means that a driver would, for example, begin his shift on Monday, work for five days and have three days off. The following week, his first shift would begin on a Tuesday with his days off falling on Sunday Monday and Tuesday before starting once more on a Wednesday and so forth.

Then, of course, there are the different types of LGV vehicles which range from 3.5 tonnes (category B) to 7.5 tonnes (category C1) further on to 32 tonnes rigid (C) and onwards to 44 tonnes articulated (C+E) and beyond.

There are many sub-categories in between and many variations but those stated above are what you will most commonly see on the highways of Great Britain. Each different type of vehicle is suited to a different kind of work. You wouldn't send a 44-tonne articulated truck onto a remote industrial unit at the far end of a country lane to pick up one pallet of crisps, in the same way, that you would not send a 3.5-tonne van into a regional operations centre to collect 10 tonnes of sheet steel. The first would be a waste of fuel and logistically difficult if not impossible, the second would just be utterly illegal.

Generally speaking, the larger the vehicle, the fewer the drops. Most 44-tonne articulated vehicle drivers make an average of between one and 5 drops per shift. In the mid-1990s when I first began driving 3.5-tonne vans, I was making around 125 drops per day. Looking back on it, I'm still astonished by that figure. I barely had enough time to scratch my own backside and I could often be found dashboard dining (eating on the move) but times have since changed. Back then, the 3.5-tonne van was not classed as an LGV vehicle and therefore the driver was not subject to tachograph rules or enforced driving hour regulations.

Most trucks on our roads today fall into one of three main categories. Box (rigid) sided vehicles or trailers, curtain-sided vehicles or trailers and flatbed vehicles or trailers. In times gone by, the flatbed type was most common. This of course meant that the driver would have to cover his load with a canvas sheet to prevent it from getting wet and then rope that sheet to the floor of the trailer. This took time, skill and created a not inconsiderable amount of inconvenience and so the curtainsider was born. With this type of vehicle or trailer, the driver must still strap his load to the bed but at least he is less likely to get soaked and muddy doing so.

Today, box vehicles and trailers are probably the most common and the easiest to load. The sides of the vehicle or trailer act as an effective form of sideways restraint in the way that curtainsiders do not (unless the curtains are of the reinforced type). The load can be secured by straps or bars running from side to side and if done correctly will prevent movement of the cargo in all directions.

Other variations on these three main themes will include, refrigerated vehicles or trailers, bulk tippers, container lorries and many more besides. Any lengthy trip along a busy motorway will reveal to the casual observer the sheer variety of trucks on our roads and an experienced driver will know how to operate most of them. Within different categories and types of vehicles, you will also have different brands of equipment with extraordinarily little standardisation between them. It is no wonder these days that most larger haulage firms employ a full-time driver trainer. There is a lot to learn and a driver can spend a lifetime learning it but still be surprised by something new almost every day.

As a driver, when it comes to choosing the type of work which would best suit, in accordance with one's licence, the driver should ask himself this question. What is more important to me? Money, or having a life?

That is really all there is to it, the reality is that clear cut because most drivers cannot have both. Balancing this job with any kind of home or social life is a little like spinning plates, eventually, something has to give.

Being at work for up to fifteen hours per day, three times per week leaves only nine hours in that day in which to commute home, eat, shower and sleep before returning to work the next morning. For some, it is preferable to tramp during the week so that the daily commute is avoided, allowing for more rest but of course this means that they do not see their family for five days out of seven.

Tramping can be better paid, as can night work. Some drivers are paid by the hour, others are salaried with bonuses on top for night-time working, tramping, working more than a certain number of hours per day, working at weekends and bank holidays etc. But all of these actions lead up to one thing, money in the bank but no opportunity to spend it.

Most trunking work (long-distance driving usually involving only one or two drops) is carried out at night and is considered to be pretty effortless. The roads are empty, the traffic minimal. When arriving at his destination, the driver rarely touches the load and occasionally doesn't even get to see it since trunking often involves taking one trailer of cargo to a depot and returning with another. The driver is however most likely to encounter road closures and lengthy diversions at night since this is when the majority of road maintenance work is undertaken.

Day work, however, is a different animal. The pay can be less and the driver is often expected to work a shorter day though a far greater amount of physical effort will usually be required. Day work may involve making deliveries to stores, manually unloading the cargo at the side of the road using a tail-lift or reversing onto unfeasibly awkward loading bays without hitting the parked cars of shoppers that probably shouldn't be there in the first place.

Day work usually involves early morning starts and early finishes but the driver does get to enjoy a life (of sorts). He may, however, on an evening out with friends at the weekend, find him or herself wanting his bed long before the night is over for everyone else.

Not only are there many different types of trucking work, there are also several different ways of being employed. These are as follows:

Employed by a company.
Employed by an agency (directly or indirectly).
Owner driver.

Let's begin with what it is like to be employed by a company. This entails being a PAYE employee, often salaried and paid monthly. The wages are usually less than an agency driver can make in an average month. You will be provided with a basic rate which can be topped up with overtime money (for working over a certain number of hours on any given day) shift allowance (for working nights) or weekend working rates. You may also receive money for doing 'nights out' and you are normally provided with a company uniform, pension, sick pay, holiday pay, free CPC training, free medicals and other benefits.

You will often be going to the same places every week and will usually be provided with maps, advice and 24/7 support. However, when you are a company driver, you have a lot less freedom. You do not often get to choose the days, shifts or hours that you work. You are expected to maintain high standards and set a good example for the company. Basically, your arse is theirs and for all of that privilege, you must pay the price. They don't quite expect you to sell them your soul but larger companies do make you feel a little bit like a very small cog in a very large machine. If you wish to be considered more than just a 'bum on a seat' it is better to opt for a smaller organisation with fewer drivers.

Agency employment is a very different animal altogether and preferred by some for its variety and flexibility. The driver is paid weekly at an hourly rate, has a say in who he wishes to work for and can dictate exactly what kind of work he is willing to do. He gets to decide his hours, days and shift patterns. However, the agency driver does not necessarily receive holiday pay, is very unlikely to receive sick pay, the pension on offer will be in the form of auto-enrollment and he will probably have to provide his or her own uniform. Additionally, he or she will usually have to pay for their own annual driver CPC course (Certificate of Professional Competency) and pay for their 5-yearly medical once they reach the required age. A good agency will provide help, advice and support for the novice and freedom and flexibility for the experienced driver. Be aware, there are good agencies, bad agencies and not much in between. The general rule of thumb though is, the smaller the agency, the more likely they are to value their drivers.

As an agency driver, you can be taxed under PAYE or Umbrella. Until recently being a Limited Company entity was also an option but that is no longer the case unless you are an owner-driver. If you are PAYE, the agency is your employer and it hires you out to any company which requires a driver. Umbrella is where your Income Tax and National Insurance is paid by a company which is separate from the agency which provides you with your work. This enables the driver to work for more than one agency without having to pay more tax than is necessary.

Limited Company is no longer permitted for any driver who does not own their own vehicle (on paper, at least) and does not possess a Transport Manager's CPC and Operators licence or who is not managed by any group or individual who does possess a Transport Manager's CPC and Operators Licence but a Limited Company driver used to be responsible for paying their Corporation Tax, Income Tax and National Insurance and managing their own financial affairs. They also had to be of good financial standing, with no outstanding bankruptcies against their name and be registered with Companies House.

The last category is that of Owner Driver. This is a trucker who owns a truck (either in fact or on paper) and has access to suitable premises where the vehicle is kept. He is usually considered to be (at the very least) a Limited Company entity and if so, the same rules previously mentioned apply. He must either have a Transport Manager CPC and Operators Licence or his operation must be managed by someone who does. He organises his own work or is provided with work by an agency or contract company and is responsible for his own tax and financial affairs. He must pay for his own training, equipment and depending upon his type of operation, may also be responsible for the maintenance and roadworthiness of his vehicle, buying his own fuel and much more besides. He may also employ other drivers (as many as the limits of his Operators Licence will allow). Owner Driver operations can consist of one individual or several and there is always the opportunity to expand. However, it is a great responsibility and extremely difficult for a single individual to undertake and manage without support (financial or otherwise) and most drivers instead, gravitate towards the first two options mentioned (company employee or agency employee) as these are the least demanding of the three.

TRUCK UPS!

So, several months ago, before I embarked upon the project which became this book, I contacted my trucking friends and colleagues for their stories and ideas. I was soon to become swamped with their tales of woe and humiliation within the wide and varied world of trucking. The following extended and penultimate chapter of this book is comprised of the stories which I have been unable to weave into the narrative so far, carefully re-packaged for your delight and edification. First names only have been given to prevent any possible repercussions or embarrassment which may arise as a result of their identities being known to the wider world. So here it is, the ultimate collection of driver f##k up's as told by the drivers themselves. So relax, sit back and enjoy the ride!

Adam

I used to regularly run from Newhaven to Dieppe in Normandy, France on a regular basis with a trailer full of floor tiles from a Marley's depot at Lenham (Marley being a forerunner of B&Q). This route took us through Paris through a tunnel with 'rattle poles' positioned on a gantry spanning the road ahead, which warned the driver if he was in a vehicle too high to go beneath. As we had driven this route the week before, I was familiar with the system. I slowed down and opened my window to listen for the noise of the rattle-poles touching the top of my trailer and, as before, we cleared them with ease and continued forward towards the tunnel.

Barely had the cab entered the tunnel and "WALLOP!" we came to an abrupt halt as the top of our trailer hit the roof of the tunnel.

Unbeknownst to us, they had resurfaced the road through the tunnel the week before, laying down several additional inches of tarmac and had forgotten to adjust the rattle poles accordingly.

We ended up having to be escorted back out of the tunnel with the help of several local Gendarmes who guided us to a nearby recovery yard where our curtain-sided trailer was 'cut down' into a flat-bed trailer leaving nothing but the deck and the bulkhead remaining.

We still managed to make our delivery and returned to the UK sporting our new 'convertible' though our boss was none too pleased.

Andrew

One night I pulled into a service station to park my vehicle up for a short break. I was so exhausted that I fell asleep slumped over the steering wheel. I had planned to take only a ten-minute nap though it ended up being far longer. I felt such a fool when some considerable time later I awoke to find a vehicle reversing into the parking space in front of my own. In my muzzy headed state, I thought that I had fallen asleep at the wheel while still driving and was about to crash into the vehicle ahead of me. I immediately started screaming and pumping the brake hard in an effort to prevent this imaginary catastrophe. I'm just glad that there was no one nearby to see me making an idiot of myself. I would have been mortified.

Andy

Back in the day when I was tramping, I was given a job to collect a load in Eastbourne with my curtain-sided trailer. So, off I went and arrived at this factory where they loaded me with all of this assorted garden furniture, the whole process taking around three hours.

Once loaded, I was instructed to drive to a layby just off a junction on the M6, so as you can imagine, I was beginning to wonder what on earth was going on but I thought to myself 'Well, OK, if that's what they want me to do, then that's what I will do', so off I go.

Anyway, several hours later I arrive at this lay-by where I am met by a man in a very dodgy looking tipper truck who winds down his window and shouts out "Follow me"!

By this time, I was beginning to get rather nervous about this whole arrangement but quelling my uncertainties I followed him anyway.

However, when the tipper truck pulled up to a traveller site my anxiety went into overdrive as this mean-looking giant of a man walked over to my truck, I began to think I was in real trouble but I need not have worried.

He opened the cab door, gave me a big grin and pointing to a nearby caravan said "Pop over there mate, we will sort all this out for you".

I walked over to the caravan, knocked on the door and was greeted by a lovely old lady with a pot of warm stew in the oven and bread and tea on the table.

I had a lovely meal that evening and a £50 tip for my troubles. They let me sleep overnight on the site and gave me a full English breakfast in the morning before I went on my way.

Just goes to show that you should never judge a book by its cover.

Bev

I used to drive a bulk-tipper vehicle, transporting loose loads of pea gravel. The vehicle was loaded from above and a sheet would then be pulled over the top and secured with a ratchet strap to hold it in place.

This particular vehicle had a ratchet strap which kept breaking and every time it broke, another knot was tied in it, making the strap progressively shorter. Of course, I reported this defect to my transport office and I was regularly fobbed-off with "We have one on order, it will arrive soon". This became an almost weekly excuse and every time I returned from my weekend rest there would be another knot and a shorter strap until finally, I could barely reach it.

On this occasion, the shortened strap became well and truly stuck and whilst doing everything I could think of to free it (swinging it and flapping it) I lost my temper with it and giving it one hard and final yank, the strap unexpectedly released itself. At the time, I had pitted my full weight against it and found myself horribly off-balance. I flew backwards, into a huge muddy puddle in front of the smoking shelter whilst the occupants looked on with barely contained mirth.

There is some karma to my sorry tale though, a week later my boss used that vehicle and exactly the same thing happened to him, and he too found himself unceremoniously deposited on his arse in the mud. Of course, following that incident, the strap was replaced within the week.

Brooke

My first ever vehicle breakdown was on the A14 in the middle of a roadworks contraflow. The trailer brakes had failed and would not release again so I called my employer and he rang for a recovery vehicle. The recovery guy somehow managed to ruin the gearbox of the tractor unit whilst towing it. Apparently, the gearbox had been on its way out for some time but because of this man's mistake, his employer had to pay for a new one. I thought my boss would be furious but in the end, he was absolutely delighted. One new gearbox, completely free of charge!

Danny

I became interested in trucking as a young boy, riding shotgun in my father's truck during school holidays but it was the demise of my chosen career that persuaded me to select haulage as a vocation. It was the late 1990's and in those years, fatalities on UK roads were at an all-time high though, despite this, the open road beckoned. I had a mortgage to pay and mouths to feed so with some redundancy money and a small loan from my local job centre I took LGV lessons, finally passing my test in 1999.

I soon discovered that I loved the work, I found the infinite variety and ever-changing scenery relaxing and although my career has been peppered with minor incidents and collisions there have been only three occasions when I truly believed I was about to meet my maker.

One of these incidents occurred when the ink on my licence was less than two years old and I was driving an eighteen tonne rigid for Walkers Crisps. On this particular day, I was given a route involving three drops in North Devon which included Barnstable, Ilfracombe and Minehead. My boss told me to take the A39 between the last two drops, adding conspiratorially "You may be able to see the

Welsh coast if it's sunny" so, with happy thoughts in my head, I set off.

I had spent much of my childhood exploring North Devon during school breaks and was looking forward to the day ahead. My route was to include the M5, M361 and the dreaded Porlock Hill, which climbs upward from east to west at a 1 in 4 gradient (25%) from the village of Porlock and is notorious for being the steepest A-road in the UK.

The forecast for the day was sunny and blustery, though once I had finished my first two drops and began to turn my attention towards my third and final delivery at Minehead, the weather started to take a turn for the worse.

As I began the long winding descent into Lynton the rain began to fall more heavily and after navigating the small narrow streets of Lynmouth I found myself at the bottom of the desperately exposed coast road where I paused and drew breath. The view ahead was disturbing in the extreme, not quite the North Face of the Eiger but a bloody steep climb nonetheless and with nowhere to turn around and little shelter from the oncoming storm, I had little choice but to proceed.

The rain was now coming in the form of heavy, sharp bursts and the wind was swirling around me from every direction at once. In no time at all, I found myself in a terrifying situation. The vehicle began to lift from the offside with every gust of wind. I could see the vast Atlantic Ocean to my left which grew further away, the higher I climbed. It then appeared to vanish altogether as I headed towards the eye of the storm.

The vehicle lifted several times as I battled in vain to keep control and with only four pallets of crisps left on board, there was almost no weight at all with which to anchor my vehicle to the road.

My vehicle clipped the crash barrier at least once, each time I noted with horror I found myself staring at a drop of more than 500ft into the churning water below. By this time, I no longer cared about the dents to the bodywork or the potential reprimand which would arise as a result of my 'carelessness'. Realising there was little oncoming traffic, I chose to occupy the other side of the carriageway at this point and hug the grass bank in the hope that it would provide some safety. However, a large pothole inconveniently positioned caused me to oversteer and the vehicle to veer wildly towards the barrier once more. Recovering control at the last possible moment, I considered my options, continue or turn back but with nowhere to manoeuvre an 18-tonne truck, I was left with no choice, so continue I did.

Just as I thought things couldn't get any worse, I saw lights ahead and could hear the distant tone of a sounding horn. At this moment I was once again positioned on the wrong side of the road and I realised that I was about to be faced, head-on, with an oncoming left-hand drive coach which was fast approaching. Hyperventilating and with a knot of terror residing in my stomach, I had no choice but to return to my side of the carriageway. At this point, I was praying there would be no backdraft from the proximity of both vehicles passing one another, which would be capable of literally sending me over the edge into the abyss below, so reciting a 'hail Mary' or two, I gripped the wheel, positioned myself in my lane as best I could and prayed.

The seconds that followed appeared to pass almost in slow motion and as the vehicle full of German tourists drew level, I glanced across at the driver. Our eyes locked and in that moment, I realised he was as terrified as I was. Fortunately, the howling wind eased and both our vehicles held fast to the tarmac and we moved past each other without incident.

At the top of Porlock Hill, the road turned inland and a layby appeared, mirage-like, from out of the storm. Gratefully, I pulled over, turned off the engine and slumped over the wheel, a quivering wreck. Within fifteen minutes, the storm had cleared and I was able to continue on my route, vowing never to venture that way again, at least, not until the next time.

Dan

A few months into my driving career I was asked to make a delivery to Redruth in Cornwall followed by a collection of CHEP pallets from Trago Mills near Bodmin. I was often asked to make the Cornish run which was almost always a pleasure in summer, despite the narrow roads and the holiday traffic.

I made it to my first drop in good time but was faced with a significant wait as the site continued to unload and reload its own vehicles, pushing me and my load further down the queue. All the while, the weather was worsening and I could sense a storm coming. Finally, it was my turn and as I opened the curtains on my trailer, the deluge began and I was drenched from head to foot. Delivery made, I got back into the vehicle and squelched all the way to Trago Mills only to be told that there was nothing to collect and I could be on my way.

By this time, the rain was coming down sideways and as I approached the Tamar Bridge, I found to my horror that it was closed due to tunnel and bridge works and that there was a diversion in place, but where were the diversion signs? I knew that the only way around this bridge was likely to involve a detour of biblical proportions but I could find nothing to indicate which way to go, so I thought to myself 'if in doubt, follow everyone else' which is exactly what I did.

Soon I found myself above the tunnels looking down onto the bridge which was peppered with maintenance vehicles sprawled out across all four lanes. As I stopped to reorientate myself, I heard a knock on my cab door. Opening my window, I found a chap who had pulled up in a car and parked behind me.

"Are you alright drive? Do you know which way to

go?"

I explained that I wasn't local and could use a little help since the diversion signs were no longer making much sense.

"Follow me drive, I'll show you the way" he offered. So grateful was I for the assistance that I did as he requested.

By this time, the weather was hitting the floor in sheets and the wind was blowing in so hard from the south that it could almost take the flesh of your bones. I could barely see more than a few metres ahead as I clung to the tail-lights of my good Samaritan, so of course, this meant that I was paying little attention to my location until I noticed the phalanx of flashing yellow lights to the right of me.

It was only then that I realised that I was driving my truck along the footpath of the Tamar Bridge. I stopped immediately, certain I had made a terrible mistake. My good Samaritan was nowhere to be seen by this time but then I heard a voice.

"You OK Drive?"

It was one of the maintenance crew who had come to my rescue. I explained my situation and he seemed totally unfazed by my story. Turns out that diverting the traffic onto the footpath of the bridge used to be standard practice back then and I was astonished to realise that I was actually heading in the right direction.

He told me to keep to 15mph and watch the strong winds before sending me on my way along this tiny footpath with barely a few inches of space between my vehicle and the three-foot-high guard rail which was all that came between myself and a one hundred foot drop into the raging waters below.

By this time it was dark, blowing a hooley and I could barely see through the rain hammering onto my windscreen. I could feel my vehicle lifting upon its axels with almost every gust of wind but I made it to the toll booth at the other end in one piece.

I was greeted by the toll booth attendant who took my money, grinned at me like a Cheshire cat and said "Bet you need a new pair of pants after all that. It's been great entertainment watching you lot coming over my bridge."

I gave him the cash and went on my way, relieved to be back on firm ground. I was never diverted that way again and can only assume that the Tamar Bridge diversion these days is somewhat more sedate and less of a white knuckle ride affair.

Dave

I used to drive RORO trucks (also known as Hookloaders). These are vehicles that carry a detachable skip or open-topped container and are often used by refuse companies to transport waste.

Early one morning I was parked up in front of a site, waiting for it to open and realised that I really needed to poop. I was carrying demolition waste and when I looked around I realised that there was nothing else for it, I was going to have to go in the back of the container.

So I used the ladder bars to climb in and jump down but once I had done the deed, I realised that I could not quite reach the ladder rungs in order to haul myself back out again.

I started banging on the back doors of the container trying to get someone's attention. I was eventually rescued by the service van driver who was wondering why my vehicle had been sat there for the past thirty minutes. I was so embarrassed didn't have the nerve to tell him why I was trapped in the back of my own truck.

David

Many years ago, I used to work for Tesco out of their Widnes depot. It was not unusual to be kept waiting at this depot for many hours for a load and I got talking to one driver who was a new starter, the ink on his licence still wet.

Following three hours of sitting on our backsides, this young chap was given his paperwork and told "Take this to Daventry".

Now, what he should have done was look at his paperwork, find the trailer number written there, hitch his tractor unit to that trailer and drive to Daventry.

What he actually did was get back in his unit with only the paperwork and make a pointless journey of 133 miles without his cargo. He didn't make that mistake twice.

David

I was once reversing onto a bay in an ice cream depot in Louth, Ireland. I could see the fork-lift truck near the bay but no driver, so I eased slowly back. It was then that I saw a young lad to the rear of my vehicle, guiding me as I reversed so, assuming he was the banksman, I continued until I heard an almighty crash.

Realising I had just accidentally reversed into the fork-lift truck, I got out of my vehicle intending to reprimand my 'banksman' only to discover, as he ran away laughing, that he was no banksman at all but some random stranger who thought it would be funny to watch the truck driver reverse haplessly into the forklift truck!

David

Back in the early 1980s, I worked as a full-time police officer and a part-time truck driver. One nightshift whilst working in my capacity as a constable, I was radioed through an incident concerning an overturned truck close to WM Dobson in Edinburgh (a long since gone haulage company, primarily involved with the transportation of Scotch Whisky to the south of the UK).

Upon arrival, I saw the vehicle with its flatbed trailer lying on its side with its once roped and sheeted cargo of canned beer, scattered all over the cobbles. Another Dobson's vehicle, still upright and intact was parked on the road a few yards ahead.

After some searching, I located both drivers huddling in the onsite drivers' room, one of whom had a badly lacerated hand but still refused to go to the local hospital.

It finally came to light that our two heroes had been tasked with delivering trailers loaded with a new product from a local brewery to storage at Dobson's yard prior to national launch.

The problem had arisen because on each trip to the cannery, they had been rewarded with a pint of 'Pundy' (a potent local ale) and they were just completing trip number eight when the incident occurred and the vehicle performed its victory roll.

The driver responsible was eventually breathalysed, the result being a foregone conclusion but I was now faced with the dilemma of how to remove twenty tonnes of alcohol and a badly bent articulated truck from the road before morning rush hour.

A tractor shovel (a vehicle that looks like a farm tractor with a big shovel on the front end) was found in Dobson's yard but the only person trained to operate it was the driver of the other vehicle who was just as inebriated as the driver who crashed his truck.

The transport manager arrived at this point and in the interests of practicality, certain matters were conveniently ignored and the driver got to work. However, progress was too slow and the manager was forced to make a statement which I suspect may haunt him to this day.

"Help yourselves, lads, the load is a write-off".

Like a rampaging plague of locusts, everyone present from roadworkers to passing commuters, office cleaners and police officers got stuck into the clearance effort.

My abiding memory is off a police car driving away from the scene so heavily loaded that its headlights were pointing at the sky and of a double-decker bus, which had been held up at the scene, also leaving laden to the limit.

The partly filled bulk tipper was taken away and 'quarantined' by the loss adjuster and the transport manager later informed me that the police had probably cleared even more away than the tractor shovel.

Even the site's mechanics managed to stash some of the prize away and routinely disappeared from their daily duties, reappearing later having developed a mysteriously rosy glow.

One of our colleagues who was not present at the time of the incident was totally underwhelmed when we later presented him with a consolation prize of four cans of the yet-to-be-released brew. His response was unrepeatable. Oh, how we laughed! Sympathy does not figure highly in the psyche of the police force.

David

Several years ago I found myself parked up for the

night on what used to be the old cattle market grounds in Doncaster.

My vehicle was positioned next to a bank that led down to the river and on this occasion, I decided to stay in my truck and watch a really good Dracula horror movie on DVD. I pulled the curtains part-way around and settled in for the night. I was just getting into the film and at the moment it reached a really scary bit when I saw a dark shape moving close my side window and heard a noise near to my cab door. Well, I was so tense at that moment that I just about jumped out of my skin, letting out a blood-curdling scream in the process.

In reply, I heard a muffled cry, as an unwary female passer-by, startled by my yelps of alarm, lost her footing on the slippery ground outside and tumbled down the bank towards the river.

The poor girl ended up bruised, shaken and covered head to toe in mud. I think it would be fair to say that it certainly put an abrupt end to her night out on the town.

Gareth

On one occasion, very early in my trucking career, I was sent out with an experienced driver whose job it was to train and guide newbies.

On this particular day, we went out fully loaded and our route took us along a fast, straight rural A-road with a low bridge. I glanced across at him as we approached and asked him if it was OK. He replied "Yeah, we fit underneath it" so on we went without incident.

Anyway, we unloaded and returned to the depot along the same road. I'm flying along quite happily at 50mph, my trainer is reading the paper and as we approached within a few yards of the bridge he looks up and yells in a panicked voice "The weight is off her, she'll be sitting high!!"

Terrified, I can do nothing by this time so I just brace myself, waiting for the impact. Of course, the truck just sails smoothly beneath the bridge and my 'trainer' is just sitting there in the passenger seat, grinning to himself.

That was a pretty mean trick to play on a new driver who hasn't yet learned about self-levelling suspension. He laughed at me about that for a very long time.

George

I once despatched a young driver for a delivery at Thornton-Cleveleys (a suburb of Blackpool) which was a short distance of less than a thirty minutes' drive away from our depot.

The moment he drove out of our depot, I received a call from the delivery point asking them when he would arrive, of course, I was pleased to be able to tell them that he would be with them post-haste. Two hours later, he had still not arrived. Shortly after, I received another phone call, this time from the driver himself.

"Boss, I think I've made a mistake" was his opening line.

He wasn't kidding. As he left the depot, he had only glanced at his paperwork. Noticing the word 'Cleve.....' he had assumed that he was making a delivery to a depot at Clevedon in Somerset, a journey of more than 200 miles away.

Astonishingly, he turned the vehicle around at the next motorway junction and still managed to make it to his delivery point in Thornton-Cleveleys before the depot closed. I think he learned a valuable lesson that day. Always check the paperwork before you leave!

Glenn

I was still a rookie driver with only thirteen weeks of trucking experience under my belt when I was asked to deliver to a Morrisons supermarket depot with a notoriously difficult loading bay.

Well, I started reversing onto it, taking my time and not getting into a panic. I was quite proud of myself for remaining so calm, I even had an audience watching me and even though it took me about ten attempts to back onto the bay, I received a little cheer and a round of applause when I finally made it.

That done, I got out of the cab and walked over to the warehouse office with my paperwork. Well, you can imagine my despair and embarrassment when they opened up the bay doors and I realised that I had not opened the barn doors of my trailer before backing onto my bay.

I received quite a few jeers and catcalls as I performed the walk of shame back to the truck, pulled it forward off the bay, opened the doors and reversed it back on again. Had to put up with a lot of teasing over that.

Graham

I used to deliver scaffolding supplies to various sites around the UK comprising of large planks of wood, metal poles and various other fixings. These all had to be secured to the bed of the trailer using heavy-duty ratchet straps. Now, these straps can be separated into two parts, one small part which consists of a hook, a short strap and a ratchet mechanism and the other part which consists of a very long strap and a hook.

If you have ever wondered how truckers get their straps over their load, this is how it is done. The part with the hook and the long strap is rolled up into a coil and whilst holding onto the non-hooked end, the coil with its hook in the centre, is thrown over the top of the load where, with luck, it should neatly fall over the load and land on the other side. Of course, before this is accomplished, it is rather important to check that no one is walking around near the opposite side of the vehicle since a flying strap with a heavy-duty hook attached to one end of it, can do rather a lot of damage.

On one particular occasion, however, unbeknownst to me, one of the staff members at a depot I was collecting from had just parked their car, on the opposite side of my trailer whilst I was distracted and unaware of what they had done. I began throwing the straps over my load, working my way along from front to back. I was about half-way along the length of my trailer when I heard an almighty crash as the hook of my strap flew straight into the middle of his rear windscreen. He was none too impressed.

Jason

I would like to recall a time when I was in Starcross (near Exeter, Devon).

Now, there is a road, quite close to the train station which is extremely narrow, along which there is a set of traffic lights and, at the time I was there, a set of roadworks which constricted the width of the road even further.

On this occasion, I had been sat at these lights for some considerable time, unable to proceed past the restriction since no one was allowing me through. Eventually, a space opened up and I moved forward only to be greeted by a very impatient driver ahead of me, blocking my route and refusing to allow me through.

This 'stand-off' continued for several minutes with the small car refusing to reverse back towards the passing point and with me being unable to reverse due to the number of vehicles which had piled up behind me.

This resulted in the passenger exiting the said vehicle and presenting me with the most fantastic display of verbal road rage, ranting about how she was calling my employer with the intention of getting me fired but what could I do? I was unable to move in any direction.

After several minutes of this tirade, I was approached by another car driver and I braced myself for more abuse, however, I was surprised and relieved when the lady gave me her number and told me she had just captured the entire incident on dash-cam and if I required any witnesses, she was more than willing to help and so, in spite of Mr and Mrs road-rage, and because of this lady's camera footage, I kept my job and my boss actually complimented me for my calm and professional manner.

Jim

I used to drive a tanker, collecting human waste from septic tanks. I should probably point out here that I am anosmic and have no sense of smell whatsoever.

Anyway, one day I pulled into the weighbridge near Halifax and noticed that there was someone new in the office.

I would normally wait in line for some considerable time before being directed onto the weighbridge but today I was rushed through. It was warm and sunny that day and I left the site rather pleased that the whole process had been completed so rapidly. It was only later that I discovered the reason for their super efficiency. It had less to do with the presence of the new office manager and more to do with the presence of the twenty tonnes of human waste inside my tank which proceeded to thoroughly nauseate everyone in the vicinity. Apparently, the smell of my cargo lingered for days!

John

I was still a newbie and was tasked to do a local delivery with a lorry load of palletised and shrink-wrapped foodstuffs. These comprised of several pallets of bottled water for one place and a few pallets full of soups and gravy granules for another place.

Anyway, back then I didn't really know how to load and strap particularly well and in such a way that the goods wouldn't shift or fall in transit.

On route to my first delivery, I was approaching a junction when a vehicle emerged from a turning ahead, cutting across my path. I hit the brakes suddenly and to my horror, felt and heard my cargo move significantly.

I arrived at my delivery point to find that the water bottles had fallen and burst open, damaging and mixing with the gravy granules. The back of my truck looked like an explosion in a Toby Carvery! Took me hours to get it all clean again.

Karl

I was once asked to transport a piece of glass from Lancashire to London for installation into a cellar skylight.

Now, this piece of glass weighed about half a tonne and when I enquired how it was going to be removed at the other end, I was simply told "Don't worry about it, they will sort all of that out when you get there".

So off I went, down to London, arrived at the site, put myself on break and watched them mess around with this thing for about two hours, trying to get it off the back of the truck.

Eventually, they got it into a couple of slings and lifted it over the side, then disaster! The glass slipped in the sling, hit the side of the truck and shattered into a million pieces.

After that, I made myself pretty scarce. Apparently, it was the second time they had done that in a week. I still chuckle about it.

<u>Kenni</u>

Back in 1981, I was training for my test. In those days it was normal to share the vehicle with another trainee as well as the instructor since some vehicles were able to take three people instead of the usual two.

So on the day of our test, I went out with the examiner first and managed to pass without too much difficulty. My training buddy, however, was extremely nervous so I tried to calm him by telling him "Don't worry, just follow what the instructor says, stay focused and you will be fine."

Anyway, about ten minutes after leaving the test centre, they were back. It turns out that whilst they were driving along MacMullen Road in Darlington, the examiner had asked his student to go straight across the roundabout and the guy had taken him at his word and driven right over the centre of it. Suffice to say, he did not pass his test that day.

<u>Kirsty</u>

I used to drive a kerbside recycling collection truck, spending my days collecting metal, glass and paper. There was another vehicle that shared our round collecting the cardboard and plastic and although we were both employed by the same company, we rarely met since we began and ended our day at different times.

On this occasion though we unexpectedly found ourselves sharing the same junction. I was preparing to turn right from a minor onto a major road and the other vehicle was on the major road, preparing to turn left onto the minor road from which I was emerging.

In my effort to be more helpful towards my trucking colleague, I exited wide from the junction so that he would have more space available to him as he entered, unfortunately, it is often said that the road to hell is paved with good intentions and as my vehicle turned right in close proximity to the opposing kerb, it met with the overhanging roof of a rather solid bus-stop. Truck, bus-stop and pride were well and truly dented that day and I didn't live it down for some considerable time afterwards.

Mark

I used to work for a company delivering to bars and restaurants in the centre of London. One time, I had to make a delivery to a Pizza Express but it was too early and they hadn't yet opened so I parked the vehicle, set the tachograph onto break mode and went to get a paper from the local newsagent.

Arrived back at the truck to find the back doors of my vehicle open and surrounded by policemen with dogs and guns.

Turns out I had created something of an incident when I unwittingly parked outside the front of the Mi5 building and walked away. Oops!

Matt

My boss once sent me to the Lee Mills area of Devon with an artic full of fertiliser.

I was using a sat-nav and checked the address before leaving so knew it was going to be a tough one but as I got closer to the farm, the roads were getting more and more narrow.

I was becoming concerned so I stopped and called the farm but they assured me that it was fine, I was on the right road and that they had trucks delivering to them all time.

I had to squeeze past a stone cottage on a corner, then a ninety-degree left-hand turn, all the while thinking to myself 'I hope I don't have to come back this way too'!

Finally, I arrived and the farmer took one look at my truck and said "Well, that's the first time we've ever had an artic in here, we usually get our deliveries on the back of a rigid".

This was truly not what I wanted to hear. I looked around their yard, thinking all the while 'Where am I going to turn around?' I was imagining having to be airlifted out by helicopter but in the end, I had to turn around in a field with the farmer on stand-by to drag me out with his tractor if I got stuck.

Ended up on a twelve-mile diversion back to the main road as I had no intention of returning the way I had arrived.

Richard

I was reversing into a very small, very winding, loading area in deepest, darkest Cornwall when I heard an ominous 'clunk'.

It turns out that whilst reversing over a little bump, my tail-lift catch had failed and the deck of the tail-lift had dropped down, effectively making my truck approximately four feet longer than it normally is. I had then proceeded to accidentally reverse into the side of a house, actually moving its wall about two inches eastwards. Not a cheap fix and I was definitely not popular that day!

Rob

I work for a breakdown company, repairing and sometimes recovering broken-down trucks.

On one occasion, I attended a breakdown where I needed to tilt the cab. (This is a mechanical process whereby the cab is lifted and tilted forward to gain full access to the engine).

Before doing this, I checked with the driver to make sure that there was nothing loose inside the cab which could cause damage if not secured and he assured me that it was all fine so I began the process.

To perform a full cab tilt, you must be standing at the side of the vehicle so I was alarmed when I heard a yell as the front of the cab windscreen shattered.

It turns out that the driver was completely unaware that the guy he was double-manning with had gone back into the vehicle for a quick nap on the bunk only to experience a very rude awakening! Not only did they have to wait for me to repair their vehicle, but they also had to wait for another guy to turn up with a new windscreen. Not a good day for either of them.

Sam

I would like to tell you about a really amazing experience I had whilst delivering to Southampton on a really hot summer's day.

I was transporting a refrigerated artic full of fresh fruit and veg to a hotel venue. It was my last drop of the day and late afternoon so as I pulled up to the loading area and opened my trailer doors, the waft of cool air coming out of the back was most welcome indeed.

On that day, there was a wedding reception being held at the venue and I was being closely watched by the groom who was standing around the rear of the bay having a smoke. After a few minutes, he asked if he could stand inside the trailer to cool down, I told him 'Yes, of course' and within a short time he was being joined by others in the group, all decked out in their wedding attire.

After making my delivery I returned to find about a dozen people, all crammed into my trailer. The wedding photographer managed to snap an awesome picture of them all, sat around on pallets in the back of my waggon.

What a fantastic way to end a hot summer's day but even now, I wish I had managed to get a copy of that photograph.

Shayne

I used to work for a company that provided exhibition equipment and support for international events.

One week, we had two major exhibitions running on the same day, one was in Greece and the other was in Spain.

Someone messed up and sent the Spanish-loaded vehicles to Greece and the Greek-loaded vehicles to Spain.

Suffice to say, both events had to be cancelled. I would not like to have been the guy who was in charge of planning that week.

Steven

Eighteen months ago as a very new driver, I found myself delivering to an Aldi RDC (Regional Distribution Centre). I had never been to this site before but all was going well at first. I found the place without any difficulty, drove through security and reversed onto the bay without any problems. Like most site's, they used a traffic light system on the loading bay meaning that when the green light shows it is safe to back up to the bay and to pull your trailer away from the bay but when the light is red it means that someone has opened your trailer door and is unloading your vehicle.

Anyway, I had been sat in my truck, parked on this bay for about two hours. My light was still green, indicating that no one had even started unloading my vehicle. I was beginning to get pretty fed up with this and got out of my cab to talk to a group of drivers who were standing around moaning about how long they had been waiting for their trucks to be unloaded.

It was only then that I found out that I was supposed to go into their warehouse and open their bay door, the roller shutter door on my trailer and put down the loading ramp myself before they would even consider touching my load! No one had told me this or trained me how to do it. As you can imagine, I was fuming. It was another hour and a half before I finally left that site! All that waiting for a delivery comprising of only two pallets!

<u>Steve</u>

I had only recently passed my test for my Category C LGV Licence and I found myself being sent to a lot of very tight, nerve-wracking places where the locals say things like "I don't know what you're worried about mate, we've had bigger trucks than yours down here".

One particular day, whilst driving my tri-axel rigid, I had to deliver to a farm in the middle of no-where. As I was getting closer and closer to the site, the road was becoming narrower and narrower until I had gone past the point where it would be a straightforward procedure for me to back out. Each turn was becoming smaller and tighter for my vehicle so I voice dialled the office and they assured me that everything was fine and that they sent vehicles into this place every day. Still, I was not reassured and as I made the next turn, I hit a low hanging tree branch, denting the roof and bringing a huge limb of the tree crashing to the ground behind me. By this time I was driving half on the road and half on the grass bank but finally, I made the final last onto a bridge and pulled into the farmyard. The owner took one look at my vehicle and said "Holy crap! It normally arrives in a van"!

It had taken me over an hour to cover the five and a half miles to this place from the main road. I unloaded the goods, turned the truck around and beat a hasty retreat.

The tree limb I had felled with the roof of my vehicle had later to be removed from the grass bank with a chainsaw, I dented the truck's fuel tank and sidebars, lost a mirror in the hedgerow and significantly scratched and dented the paintwork.

The route planner at our site was given a disciplinary and I learned a very valuable lesson. If it doesn't look right or doesn't feel right, ignore what the idiots in the office have told you, turn around while you still can and get the hell out!

DRIVE IT LIKE
A GIRL

It is estimated that less than twenty percent of those involved in the haulage industry are women. This figure includes management, warehouse and administrative staff. Somewhere between two and five percent of that total figure would include lorry drivers.

Although haulage, in one form or another, has existed since the days when it has been necessary to move goods over long distances from point A to point B, the steam-powered lorry was not invented until the mid-1800s.

Daimler was the first to create a diesel-driven heavy goods vehicle in 1896 and since then, the industry has gone from strength to strength.

The first heavy goods vehicle driving test in the UK did not come about until 1934 and (from what I can ascertain) was not at the time a mandatory requirement for all lorry drivers as some inherited what is known as 'grandfather rights', meaning that because they were already experienced drivers, a test was not required of them.

During the period of WW2, all driving tests (including those for heavy goods vehicles) were suspended, not to be reinstated until 1946. During this period, many women drove heavy military vehicles as part of the war effort, including our own dear Queen Elizabeth II and many decades later, her daughter Anne, the Princess Royal, followed in her mother's footsteps, passing her HGV test in 1974.

One of the very first women to take up HGV driving as a career in the UK was a lady by the name of Rita Jane, who took on the role of driver for her Polish husband's potato merchant business in the late 1950s. It is believed she did not hold a full licence and probably received very little training before taking to life on the road, regularly clocking up to one hundred hours per week and often accompanied by her young daughter.

It isn't only the haulage industry which has often excluded women from its ranks.

Careers in engineering, the sciences, mathematics and many more besides, were closed to the majority of women until after the war years had been and gone. Often our achievements before these times were ignored or overwritten by those who record our histories. Today, women's accomplishments are still overlooked and neglected in favour of their male colleagues. If you think that a google search would find these 'lost' heroines of the industrial world, think again. History is written with a male bias and many female achievements are either forgotten or deliberately erased from the record. Believe it or not, there is still at least one private club in London which actively excludes women from its membership and female guests are only permitted to access certain areas within the establishment.

It is worth bearing in mind that men did not see women in this country as being fit to own property until 1870 or to vote on equal terms, regardless of class or wealth, until 1928, a right which most men had enjoyed for ninety-six years with the passing of the 1832 reform act.

Haulage is still regarded as a male-dominated industry and at least for now, that is certainly the case with seventy percent of all senior management roles within the industry being held by men.

So how does this affect the reality of doing a job where you are one of only a handful of female drivers if not the only female driver?

In my opinion, unless you are employed by a major industry leader which prides itself on fair, equal and unbiased policies and conditions for all of its staff, you will often find yourself at a disadvantage.

In all but my most recent past, I have been regularly offered contracts that paid less than those offered to my male colleagues. Added to that, I have often been expected to work harder for it with little regard to my desired shift patterns or working preferences. I have never married and have always lived child-free and from this perspective alone, I cannot clearly see how any woman with children would manage unless they had a partner who either worked from home or had a very understanding employer when it came to childcare arrangements. The responsibility of caring for children and elderly relatives often falls to women. This is, unfortunately, a fact, even in this modern age and it must change if women are ever to punch through that glass ceiling and take their rightful place as leaders of their field.

Although we have come a long way in the last fifty years, we still have some distance to travel before all that we achieve is considered 'ordinary' or 'everyday' and equal to that of our male peers.

Whenever women have moved into an industry from which they have been previously excluded, the rights and conditions of the workers within that industry have improved exponentially. Simply put, women make things happen and we do not settle for less than what is our due.

As it stands, conditions for truck drivers are hardly ideal. When a trucker leaves their house to go to work, they often have no idea of when they will see their own front door again. The work holds very little consistency or predictability and home life always has to take a back seat.

It's little wonder that women do not see haulage (and particularly truck driving) as a desirable industry.

And yet it has been proven time and time

again that women make better truck drivers than men. We take fewer risks than our male counterparts. We prioritise safety over speed. We plan strategically and are more likely to spot potential hazards further in advance and in a recent survey it was shown that whilst little over three percent of female LGV drivers had points on their licence for speeding, the figure was double that for men.

Even industry employers will concede that a used vehicle predominantly driven by a woman is usually found in better condition, internally and externally, than one driven predominantly by a man, so the haulage industry would do well to promote the recruitment of women into its ranks.

Unfortunately, haulage is one of these old fashioned industries where most people begin at the bottom (usually as a warehouse worker or drivers' mate) and work their way up the ladder into management. Because most of the starting roles often involve hard manual labour, many women are deterred, not wishing to appear physically inferior to their male colleagues and opt for administrative roles instead. These roles involve learning skills that can often be transferred from one industry to another and are not specific to haulage so many young women who begin within this industry, do not necessarily remain within this industry.

The atmosphere itself can also be somewhat intimidating to those unused to trucker humour (which can be a little rum and ribald, to say the least) and coupled with the lack of female role models within haulage, the industry is not considered an attractive one by most female school leavers.

Even the vehicles we drive are built almost exclusively by men. Most manufacturers design the seating position to suit male proportions and if you think that those of a woman would be similar to those of a man of similar height, you would be mistaken.

Firstly, the average height of a woman in the UK is 5ft 3 inches or 161 cms. For a man, the average height is 5ft 9 inches or 175 cms. The average inside leg measurement of the average man is around 30 inches, for the average woman, it is between 30 and 32 inches. So as you can see, women usually have proportionately longer legs and a shorter body. Our shoulders are also smaller and our arms shorter, further reducing our upper body reach.

At 5ft 6 inches, I am above average in height but still find it difficult to attain a comfortable driving position within a truck. The seat belt is often set too high, cutting into my neck and many of the dials and buttons on the dashboard are beyond easy reach of my fingertips. More than once it has been remarked upon that I look like a wayward child who has stolen her daddy's truck. There is, of course, also a safety issue since female drivers must position themselves closer to the steering wheel (and therefore closer to the driver's airbag) to obtain a good view over the dashboard, placing them at greater risk of being injured in a high impact RTA.

Even the steps into the cab and onto the catwalk at the rear of the cab have been spatially designed for men, as has the height of the trailer deck, the curtains of a curtain-sided trailer and the trailer door handles and locks. Don't even get me started on any of the (so-called) ground coupling systems which were surely designed by a 6 foot 6 inch tall brute of a man with the abdominal muscles of a champion wrestler.

What we lack in strength and size, we must make up for in determination and persistence. Most female truckers have over several years, much practice and many bruises, been forced to develop little tricks and workarounds to enable us to effectively perform the difficult tasks required of us in our everyday jobs. From using our knees and hips to help us insert recalcitrant air-lines, to using gloves with extra grip so that we can throw our full body weight into pulling open trailer doors, hauling heavily loaded pallet trucks and pushing disobedient cages around the deck.

Even so, in the days when I used to manually unload and reload my vehicle, I was forever covered in vicious scratches and bruises and unsure of how most of them had got there.

Then there is the clothing issue and the fact that even though we are living in the second decade of the twenty-first century, many employers do not provide truckers' uniform which is specific-ally tailored for women. At best, we are provided with what can only be described as 'unisex' cloth-ing which is in fact, suitable for no one, least of all women. The jackets, jumpers and polo shirts will be too small on the hips, not wide enough around the chest, too large across the shoulders and ri-diculously long in the arms. The trousers will be too snug around the seat, too generous around the waist and short enough in the leg to be used by a Max Wall tribute act. Any steel toe capped boots you are offered will be in a man's size, making them too wide, too heavy and as ungainly to wear as the boxes they came in. Certainly, the tailor-ing of women's workwear is rarely considered, the femininity, never.

And yet, we continue to do our work stead-ily, reliably and with little complaint regarding our treatment. We learn to ignore or even to laugh at the salty comments of other truckers and the raised eyebrows or 'double-takes' from members of the general public. We grow used to being passed over for the best contracts or the newest vehicles in favour of our male colleagues and we learn to accept that we are occasionally considered to be deficient or inferior drivers by those less en-lightened individuals in positions of management.

The life of a trucker is hard but the life of a female trucker, doubly so.

We are often expected to undertake tasks that our male equivalents would refuse to do and because of our sex, it is often thought that we are less likely to kick up too much of a fuss. To a degree, this is true and we do our gender no favours whatsoever by permitting ourselves to be taken advantage of in this way. A propensity for confrontation in the face of opposition or intimidation is not generally found in the nature or the social training of most women, though as my friends, family and colleagues would agree, I am probably something of an exception to this rule. I take no prisoners, and woebetide anyone who steps on my toes in their size ten boots!

Even in this era of equality, we are still expected to behave in a certain way, follow a career path appropriate to our gender, be women rather than who we wish to be regardless of our sex. Men are not expected to conform to such stereotypes of 'normality' nor exist with such strictures upon their freedoms and it is the idea that what is appropriate for men, is not appropriate for women, which must cease if we are ever to progress far and away from the dark old days of when a woman was not permitted to work, own property or hold a bank account without the permission of her husband or a male relative.

Unless women are brave enough to move forward into the worlds which, for too long, have been the preserve of men, we shall forever be relegated to lesser roles in life, unable and unwilling to explore what exists beyond that which our husbands, fathers and male peers have spread before us.

Yes, the life of a female trucker is tough, exasperating and sometimes terrifying but we must continue to push at the barriers of what is considered appropriate or even possible for us.

Yes, the life of a female trucker can be lonely. Women are generally more social creatures than men and truck driving is anything but social though, for many, their truck is their favourite space, their own little oasis of calm and a far cry from the micro-managed environment of the traditional female workplace. I know of many women for whom becoming a truck driver was the best decision they have ever made and all the gender barriers, prejudice and loneliness which is part and parcel of what it is to be a lady trucker is a price well paid for a life on the open road.

For all young women considering a career in truck driving, I leave you with this quote from Ruth Bader Ginsburg.

"Women belong in all places where decisions are being made. It shouldn't be that women are the exception."

EPILOGUE

Since the completion of this manuscript in May of 2021, many situations within haulage and logistics have altered dramatically. A combination of three separate sets of circumstances have created the perfect storm and we are now experiencing record-breaking levels of driver shortages. In 2015 the estimated shortfall was believed to be around 50,000. By 2020 the figure had risen to 75,000 and in 2021 it is now thought to be around 100,000. Should this continue, it is estimated that this figure will reach 150,000 by 2023. Three recent events have meant that many European truckers are deserting the UK in their droves and some British drivers are walking away from trucking altogether.

Firstly, Brexit and the uncertainty surrounding any leave to remain, which may or may not be granted to non-British citizens, caused some to simply cut their losses and return to their home countries. Then along came Covid-19 and those with families in Europe returned home for fear of being stranded in the UK for many months on end. The third and final blow was IR35 which came into force in April 2021. This is a governmental ruling which dictates that those who work for one company as a Limited Company entity or self-employed contractor, cannot consider themselves self-employed and must be classed as PAYE and subject to paying the same rate of tax as any other employee.

I can understand that this ruling has been designed to protect individuals from exploitation but there is obviously another agenda at work here, and that is to force all those who were previously considered self-employed, to pay more in Income Tax and National Insurance contributions.

Unfortunately, haulage relies heavily upon agency drivers, many of whom were greatly affected by this ruling. Those drivers who owned their own vehicles were exempt, but they were very much in the minority and those classed as Limited Company drivers who didn't own their own vehicles, were earning far higher rates than those who were PAYE and they were still able to consider so much of what they spent as tax-deductible.

There are of course ways of working around this situation (such as being an owner-driver) but this requires the driver to complete a Transport Manager CPC exam and hold an Operator's licence or to pay someone to do this for him. This is all well and good but the cost of the course comes to around £2,000, it is notoriously difficult to pass, and if English is not your first language, it could prove to be an insurmountable challenge.

The reason why many Eastern European drivers came to the UK to work in the first place, was the great disparity between British earnings and what they could make in their country of origin. If they became a Limited Company driver and lived a simple life in the UK they would earn enough to survive and have cash to spare, which could then be sent home. That money could buy them a sizable property, privately educate their children and permit their families a far greater quality of life than they could otherwise expect, and who could blame them? The British have been doing exactly that for centuries. Colonialism was based entirely upon this model and some opportunism continues to this day, if on a smaller scale. No doubt many of us could name at least one friend or relative who is paid an obscene sum of money to work in a foreign land.

This has now been greatly curtailed by the IR35 ruling since no one in their right mind wishes to hand over more of their earnings to the government than is absolutely necessary, resulting in a mass exodus back to Europe and many older British truckers deciding to retire early rather than hand over more of their hard-earned cash to the taxman.

There are 320,000 LGV licence holders in the UK and 90,000 who are not currently working as truck drivers. It is estimated that 15,000 truckers permanently left Britain in 2020 and due to Covid-19 an estimated 30,000 LGV tests could not be completed during 2020 and 2021 so we are now walking into a crisis of epic proportions.

Only time will tell how this all plays out, but something must be done and soon. Either truck drivers must be permitted exemption from IR35 or the government must grant 'skilled worker status' to truckers, enabling recruitment from overseas. Increasing permitted working or driving hours simply will not cut the mustard and could be entirely counterproductive, forcing many more to leave the industry. Drivers permitted working hours already far exceed that which would be expected of any office or factory worker and until very recently, rates of pay could be as little as £10 per hour in some parts of the UK. Some haulage firms are still offering monthly paid salaries which amount to little more than minimum wage when calculated by the hour. This situation, however, is changing and due to the current shortage, wages for truck drivers finally appear to be rising.

I have seen offers on various employment websites of £25 per hour for nighttime shifts and Sunday working or £30 per hour for bank holidays. With a predicted shortage of 150,000 drivers by 2023, the forecast is bleak for this country and the consequences, unthinkable. Already, supermarkets are daily discarding tonnes of perishable food, which they are unable to deliver due to the simple fact that they have nobody available to get it there. Should this continue, fully stocked shelves of fresh produce will become a thing of the past and should the hourly rate for drivers increase, these costs will only be passed on to the consumer resulting in price rises for which the poorest in our society will suffer most.

All I will say is "watch this space". These are indeed interesting times and if you are considering a career in haulage, right now, this country needs YOU!

Printed in Great Britain
by Amazon

81249971R00119